TEACHING MATHEMATICS AS STORYTELLING

Teaching Mathematics as Storytelling

By

Rina Zazkis
Simon Fraser University, Canada

and

Peter Liljedahl
Simon Fraser University, Canada

SENSE PUBLISHERS
ROTTERDAM / TAIPEI

A C.I.P. record for this book is available from the Library of Congress.

ISBN 978-90-8790-733-4 (paperback)
ISBN 978-90-8790-734-1 (hardback)
ISBN 978-90-8790-735-8 (e-book)

Published by: Sense Publishers,
P.O. Box 21858, 3001 AW Rotterdam, The Netherlands
http://www.sensepublishers.com

Cover drawing by Dov Zazkis

Printed on acid-free paper

All rights reserved © 2009 Sense Publishers

No part of this work may be reproduced, stored in a retrieval system, or transmitted in any form or by any means, electronic, mechanical, photocopying, microfilming, recording or otherwise, without written permission from the Publisher, with the exception of any material supplied specifically for the purpose of being entered and executed on a computer system, for exclusive use by the purchaser of the work.

TABLE OF CONTENTS

Introduction	ix
Chapter 1: A story	1
Prelude	1
What is a story?	2
Stories in the classroom	4
Stories of different kinds	4
Chapter 2: What makes a story	7
Plot	9
Conflict	12
Images	15
Human meaning	16
The sense of wonder	18
Humor	19
Patterns	20
Summary	21
Chapter 3: Storytelling	23
Storytelling by storytellers	23
Storytelling in educational context	24
Storytelling in the mathematics classroom	26
The farmer and the crow: Telling of a story	26
After the story is told	28
Chapter 4: Stories that set a frame or a background	31
Riddle of the Sphinx	31
Frame or focus?	32
Chapter 5: Stories that accompany and stories that intertwine	37
Archimedes: Making the distinction	37
Archimedes revisited: exemplifying the distinction	38

TABLE OF CONTENTS

Chapter 6: Stories that introduce	43
Anno's Mysterious Multiplying Jar: A story of factorial	44
Grains on a chessboard: A story of exponential growth	46
A fly on a ceiling: A story of Cartesian coordinates	47
Pirates and buried treasure: A story of a standard unit	48
Counting an army: A story of positional decimal system	49
Planet Penta: A story of base 5	50
Summary	51
Chapter 7: Stories that explain	51
Stories that explain a concept	51
Changing stories to clarify confusion	58
Summary	64
Chapter 8: Stories that ask a question	67
Dressing up	67
… for a party	69
Students as problem actors: King Solomon and Queen Sheba	70
Students as problem actors: The bedouin will	72
Three bears in a different story	73
Chapter 9: Stories that tell a joke	77
Warming up	78
Jokes and language	79
Jokes about mathematicians	81
Precision with a smile	83
Self reference and humour	83
Summary	84
Chapter 10: Creating a story	85
Planning framework	85
Example of planning 1 (elaborated): Area and perimeter	89
Example of planning 2 (less elaborated): Telling time	95
Example of planning 3 (abbreviated): Number properties	98
Chapter 11: Stories of a teacher and his students	101
Episode 1: Story to introduce a concept	101
Episode 2: Stories that accompany	111
Episode 3: Story that asks a question	116
Episode 4: Story to introduce an activity	116
Summary and a warning	122

Chapter 12: Using existing stories	123
Purpose	123
Script	124
Telling	125
Context	126
Using existing story books	127
Resources	136
References	137

INTRODUCTION

We like to tell stories. We tell stories about mathematics, about mathematicians, and about doing mathematics. We do this firstly because we enjoy it. We do it secondly because the students like it. And we do it thirdly because we believe that it is an effective instructional tool in the teaching of mathematics. We are not alone in this. There is ample literature to support the enjoyment of storytelling on the part of both the story teller and the story listener. There is also an abundance of anecdotal data that suggest "telling a story creates more vivid, powerful and memorable images in a listener's mind than does any other means of delivery of the same material" (Haven, 2000, p. xvii). Aside from the educational value, however, there is also beauty. There is beauty in a story well told, and there is beauty of a story that can move a listener to think, to imagine, and to learn.

But, what are the benefits for students? Marie Shedlock, a teacher who became a famous storyteller, puts this nicely.

> One might as well try to show with a pint measure how the sun and the rain have affected a plant, instead of rejoicing in the beauty of the sure, if slow, growth. The, again, why are we in such a hurry to find out what effects have been produced by our stories? Does it matter whether we know today or tomorrow how much a child has understood? For my part, so sure do I feel of the effect that I am willing to wait indefinitely. [...] The teachers of general subjects have a much easier and more simple task. Those who teach science, mathematics, even, to a certain extent, history and literature, are able to gauge with a fair amount of accuracy by means of examination what their pupils have learned. The teaching carried on by means of stories can never be gauged in the same manner. (Shedlock, 1924, pp. 130-131)

With this spirit in mind we wrote this book. We believe it is of interest for those who teach mathematics, or teach teachers to teach mathematics. It may also be of interest to anyone who ever listened to a story and learned something from it. It may be of interest to those who like stories or like mathematics. It also may be of interest to those dislike either mathematics or stories, but are ready to reconsider their position.

In this book we share with the reader many stories that we have told and that we keep telling our students. We tell stories in the mathematics classroom to achieve an environment of imagination, emotion, and thinking. We tell stories in the mathematics classroom to make mathematics more enjoyable and more memorable. We tell stories in the mathematics classroom to engage students in a mathematical activity, to make them think and explore, and to help them understand concepts and ideas.

INTRODUCTION

Furthermore, we share with the reader several techniques for storytelling that makes telling more interactive and more appealing to the learner. We also present a framework that may help potential storytellers create their own stories, as well as ideas as to how existing stories can be enriched and adapted for the needs of any particular audience. By such means we hope that more teachers and more colleagues will story-tell in their classrooms, and, like Marie Shedlock, be patient enough to wait for long-term benefits.

CHAPTER 1

A STORY

PRELUDE

Once upon a time, long ago in a land far away there lived a tribe of farmers called the Zalla. The Zalla were hard working people who were happy for all that they had. They were happy for the dark rich soil in which they grew their crops, they were happy for the rains that nourished their fields, but most of all they were happy for their sheep. They had lots of sheep. For the Zalla, the sheep were the source of warm coats, of carpets for the chilly floors of their caves and bungalows, and of tasty meat for dinner and fresh milk for breakfast. Needless to say, the sheep were very important to the Zalla.

Amzula, the chief shepherd of the Zalla tribe, was responsible for watching over the sheep. Every morning Amzula woke up before the sun rose and let the sheep out of their pens and into the pastures. The sheep explored the hills and the meadows, grazed on the green grass, breathed the crisp air, and satisfied their thirst with the fresh cold water of mountain fed streams. At dusk Amzula would call the sheep back to the safety of the pen before the fall of darkness. His most important job was to make sure that all the sheep had returned, for if any sheep were left out they might fall prey to the wild animals that prowled the hills and the meadows at night.

But here was the problem. Amzula could not count. In fact, no one in the tribe of Zalla could count. And no one in all the neighboring tribes of Agraba could count either. Not that these people were not smart, for they were. They just lived a long, long time ago, before humans knew how to count. Still, Amzula's most important job was to ensure that all the sheep returned for the night. Remember, these sheep were very important to the people of Zalla. What would you do? Is it possible, without counting, to make sure that the same number of sheep returned in the evening as left in the morning?

This question can be posed to students from elementary school to University, and from the variety of their solution attempts the idea of one-to-one correspondence will eventually emerge. That is, for every sheep exiting the pen we can put a pebble in a bowl, tie a knot, or make a mark on a shepherd's stick. Then, for every sheep that returns we can take a pebble out, untie a knot, or erase a mark, and if we are lucky the return of the last sheep will correspond with the removal of the last pebble or the erasing of the last mark.

So, what next, you would ask. It depends. With very young students a story like this may spark an awareness of the ingenuity of counting that they may have taken for granted. With older elementary school students, we would continue the story with Amzula the VI, our Amzula's great-great-great-grandchild who *could* count, but only up to ten. In helping him to assure that all the sheep got home, the students could reinvent the decimal numeration system. With students in grades 8 and 9, the ancient idea of one-to-one correspondence could lead to the concept of a function, one of the most important concepts in mathematics in general, and of the high school mathematics curriculum in particular. With University students, continuing the story of one-to-one correspondence in comparing finite sets extends naturally to the comparison of infinite sets, with some surprising results, including the fact that the set of even numbers is no smaller than the set of natural numbers.

A few of these exciting possibilities are explored in this book. For now, we just wanted tell a story in order to pave the way for the discussion of stories in the mathematics classroom.

WHAT IS A STORY?

When dealing with mathematics we may not be used to thinking in terms of telling a story. In fact, the task of learning mathematics seems quite remote from anything to do with stories. It might be that we occasionally tell a 'mathematical' story in the course of teaching children, but it is only an incidental accessorizing of the 'real work', which is often perceived as practicing the mathematical algorithms themselves. This, however, is a very shortsighted and impoverished view of the potential of stories in the teaching and learning of mathematics. It is our aim in the chapters that follow to show that through stories we can make mathematics more accessible to students, as well as more engaging.

But first let us look at what stories are and what makes them special. Words like narrative, account, yarn, legend, chronicle are listed among the synonyms that describe the meaning of story. A dictionary definition suggests that a story is "a factual or fictional account of an event or series of events". However, neither definitions nor synonyms help us understand the power of stories and their purpose. Despite the feeling that "no definition is necessary", or that "every child knows what a story is", there have been attempts to articulate what makes a story distinguishable from any other kind of a narrative. We consider two of such articulations below.

> What is a story? A compact answer is to say that it is a narrative unit that can fix the affective meaning of the elements that compose it. That is, a story is a unit of some particular kind; it has a beginning that sets up a conflict or expectation, a middle that complicates it, and an end that resolves it. The defining feature of stories, as distinct from other kinds of narratives – like arguments, histories, scientific reports – is that they orient our feelings about their contents. (Egan, 2004, 2008)

> What is a story? In essence, a narrative account requires a story that raises unanswered questions or unresolved conflicts; characters may encounter and then resolve a crisis or crises. A story line, with a beginning, middle and end, is identifiable. [...] It is generally agreed that stories are a powerful structure

for organizing and transmitting information, and for creating meaning in our lives and environments. (Green, 2004)

The common features in both descriptions are those of a conflict and a structure. (We elaborate on this in the next chapter). However, while Green's attention is mainly on the information embedded in a story, Egan's additional focus is on affect, on orienting feelings. Egan describes a story as a particular kind of narrative unit that orients our emotions to the events presented through the narration. That is, stories make us feel. And in this, stories are unique. We ascribe emotional meaning to events, and to people, and to our own lives by plotting them into partial or provisional stories. We orient ourselves emotionally to our environment by involving it in our stories. The value of the story to teaching is precisely its power to engage the students' emotions and also, connectedly, their imaginations in the material of the curriculum.

This feature of stories is perhaps easily understood in terms of the newspaper editor who asks a reporter, "What's the story on this?" The editor is obviously not asking the reporter to create fiction, but rather is asking the reporter to shape the events to bring out their emotional force. That is, the reporter is not inventing details, but rather selecting and organizing them in order to bring out the affective meaning of the topic. It is this latter sense that we are mostly concerned with.

In our description of how to teach mathematics, we are not concerned with fictional stories about the topic, but rather we are concerned with how we can shape the topic to enhance its attraction to students. In doing this, we will not be falsifying anything, or giving precedence to entertaining students over educating them. Instead, we will be engaging them. We see engaging students with mathematical activity as a crucial aspect of successful education as, and it is the real vividness and importance of this subject in which we want to engage students.

In summary, the great power of stories, according to Kieran Egan (1986, 2004, 2008), is in their dual mission: they communicate information in a memorable form and they shape the hearer's feelings about the information being communicated. Furthermore, Egan's reference to a *hearer* emphasizes that a story is being told and listened to, rather than decoded from a written text. In our discussion of story telling we first describe different shapes that a *story* may take and then focus on the *telling*.

"Telling a story is a way of establishing meaning" (Egan, 1986, p. 37). And establishing meaning should be, we believe, a central thread in teaching mathematics – a subject that is too often perceived as the manipulation of symbols, the meaning of which is often far from clear to students. Unfortunately, the telling of stories is an infrequent and seemingly off-task activity in a mathematics classroom. More often we hear stories *about* mathematics classrooms (how boring they were), *about* mathematical experiences (how humiliating they were), or *about* mathematics tasks (how pointless they were). What story can one possibly tell about long division? We do not suggest here that every lesson or every topic can be learned with a story. However, we believe that introducing stories *in* mathematics

CHAPTER 1

classrooms will change the stories *about* the mathematical experiences of learners mentioned above.

STORIES IN THE CLASSROOM

Communicating information and orienting feelings are feature of all stories – fairy tales, news reports, bedtime stories, fables or stories of historical events. Using stories in a classroom can serve many additional and different purposes. Stories may spark interest, assist in memory, and reduce anxiety. They can create a comfortable and supportive atmosphere in the classroom, and build rapport between the instructor and the students.

Creating interest with a story is an important initial step. Describing a chain of events may engage students, create excitement, mystery or suspense, and motivate thinking about a particular problem. Stories may convey passion and enthusiasm. They may also introduce ways of thinking and acting like their heroes, create empathy, and make the material more accessible and memorable. Stories in which students identify with the heroes may also make the lesson more relevant and more vivid. Stories that involve specific examples may help students relax as they provide something to hold to when moving to general theory or technical detail. In general, a classroom story can serve as a purposeful break from the routine, creating a refuge to return to and to seek more stories.

What is mentioned above about the different purposes of stories is true for any subject matter, including mathematics. What is special about the use of stories in the mathematics classroom is that they can assist in understanding difficult concepts and ideas, and assist in solving problems. According to Egan (2008), "The engaging quality of stories seems tied up with the fact that they end. Unlike history or our lives, in which succeeding events compel us constantly to reassess our feelings about earlier events, the story fixes how we should feel, and this provides us with a rare security and satisfaction." In Mathematics classroom, however, a distinguishing feature of some of the stories is that there is no traditional 'ending'.

Sparking students' initial interest with a story is not that difficult to achieve. Our goal, however, is to sustain this interest, to sustain students' engagement and not let it evaporate as the story ends. That is why some of our stories never end, some do not adhere to the 'classical' structure of beginning, middle, and end. The 'end', or conflict resolution, is often turned into student activity; the story evolves into exploration and problem solving. We exemplify this in the following chapters. In the next section we introduce several types of stories used to enhance the learning of mathematics.

STORIES OF DIFFERENT KINDS

Stories emerge in different form and kind. Some are real while others are fictional, some are written in prose while others are in verse, some make us think and others make us wonder, some make us cry while others make us laugh. There are stories that we enjoy and wish they would never end, and there are other stories that we rush to finish, eager to know how they end.

Literary genre sources distinguish between different narratives: folk tales, fairy tales, tall tales, bed-time stories, myths, legends, essays, fables, parables, and ballads. There are stories of the past and stories of current events. Initially stories developed as part of the oral culture, as the medium for preserving heritage and recording history. Later, with the development of print culture, books and newspapers became the main sources of stories. More recently, stories are presented as movies and TV programs, or even video games.

However, the discussion of literary genres, on all their varieties, is not our concern here. We are concerned with teaching and learning of mathematics, and making this subject come alive in the classroom. As such, we use stories of all the possible kinds presented in all the available media. Though 'story' is defined at times as a 'sequence of events', it is not the events that are of our interest here. We distinguish the kinds of stories not by their structure but by the kind of engagement with mathematical content the story brings.

In Chapter 4 we will consider stories that frame or provide the background for a mathematical activity. For example, if our hero has to solve a problem to save a princess, any problem appropriate for the given group of students can be embedded in this story. Then, in Chapters 5 and 6, we note that some stories end where mathematical engagement starts and some stories continue alongside mathematics. Thus, we distinguish between stories that introduce, and stories that accompany and intertwine with mathematical activity.

Mathematics is often perceived as a collection of facts and skills to be learned, and often these facts and skills are counterintuitive to the learner. When this happens a common reaction is to seek refuge in the meaningless memorization of rules. Experienced teachers can easily point to such places, places in which encounters with mathematics are most puzzling and counterintuitive for their students. Instead of reciting rules we suggest in Chapter 7 explaining rules with stories. This introduces a new kind of story – a story that explains. Division by zero, division by a fraction, and the manipulation of negative integers are but a few examples of concepts that students find hard to understand and we believe that explaining with stories will be helpful. We also demonstrate how variation on a story can help in solving a problem or gaining a better understanding of a solution.

Another kind of story is a story that asks a question. In schools today we are more familiar with the distant cousins of such stories, often called 'word problems'. These word problems start in kindergarten with apples that Jack and Jill put together and continue with tenth grade trains that leave stations at different times and aim to arrive sometime somewhere, periodically changing the speed of their travel. However, a closer look at such stories reveals that they are not really stories at all. They have been stripped of the details and emotions that help to orientate a listener's feelings. What is left is an empty shell of a story with emphasis on the question mark at its end. Ironically, such problems evolved from true stories that presented a riddle or a puzzle. It is our intention to return to these roots, at least in some problems, and to re-create the story of the word problem. We develop this theme in Chapter 8.

Furthermore, we consider a joke as a short, at times very short, story and in Chapter 9 we exemplify several jokes relevant to specific mathematical content. We discuss how jokes can help both as a pedagogical tool, and as an assessment tool.

Chapter 10 outlines a specific framework for incorporating stories in planning for instruction. Chapter 11 exemplifies how this framework was used by one creative teacher and his students. Finally, in Chapter 12 we attend to how existing stories can be shaped and modified to serve a designated group of students.

We have mentioned different kinds of stories to tell in the mathematics classroom: stories that provide a frame or background, stories that introduce, stories that accompany or intertwine, stories that ask a question, and stories that explain. Of course, very often these distinctions are overlapping as the same plot of a story may result in a different engagement of learners. This classification is neither complete nor disjoint; there are stories that do not belong to any of these categories and there are stories that comply with more than one. Furthermore, the nature of a story may change, taking on different shapes in different contexts. Stories that accompany are usually told or read by a teacher. Other kinds of stories can be started by a teacher and then completed, or at least participated in, by the learner.

We believe that telling is no less important than the story itself, and telling – to which we devote full attention in Chapter 3 – is one of the ways to shape the story. In the following chapters we explore the components of a story and the art of storytelling.

CHAPTER 2

WHAT MAKES A STORY

What is it about a story that is so engaging? Before we address this question we present the classic story of Karl Friedrich Gauss as we would tell it to our students.

Although Karl Friedrich Gauss (1777-1855) would eventually grow up to be a brilliant mathematician (some would even say the greatest mathematician), as a child he was more than a handful for his teachers. You see, at heart Karl was a happy boy who liked nothing more than to tease and play tricks on his friends. One day, while he was still quite young Gauss was being particularly jovial in class. He had finished his work early and had proceeded to disturb his classmates with his mischievous antics. One of his favourite tricks was to imitate quite ordinary, but annoying sounds. He was very good at imitating the sound of creaking wood – as in a creaking floorboard or a creaking chair. This was especially appropriate given that the school that Karl attended was very old and looked just like the kind of place that would creak and groan when people moved about. In reality, however, the school was very well built and did not at all creak. But, year after year he would torment his teachers with these sounds. As they walked around the room or sat down in a chair their every move would be accompanied by a cacophony of creaks and groaning wood joints. Some teachers took this better than others, but no one took it worse than Mr. Schmidtsenburgersnoff. Mr. Schmidtsenbergersnoff was Karl's teacher when Karl was 9 years old. He was an overbearing man who was a stickler for discipline and made no bones about dishing out severe punishments for even the slightest misbehaviours. On this particular day Mr. Schmidtsenbergersnoff was in a worse mood than usual. So, annoyed with Karl's joking around, he walked down the aisle to the back of the classroom where Karl was sitting and set a task for him that he was sure would occupy young Karl for the remainder of the day. "For your pestilence, Karl, I will ask you to add up the numbers from 1 to 100!" he barked. All of Karl's classmates were stunned into silence. This was by far the most severe punishment the teacher had ever given out. Poor Karl they all thought, this time the teacher had surely broken him. As the teacher turned to walk back to his desk at the head of the class every child in the room stared at this humourless and evil man. Just before he got to the front of the class the creaking sounds started. Mr. Schmidtsenburgersnoff spun on his heals and stared at Karl. Surely young Karl couldn't be done already. The entire class stared, their collective breath held in anticipation. "The sum is 5050!" The

CHAPTER 2

classroom erupted into laughter. Once again Karl had gotten the best of the teacher.

This was too much! Mr. Schmidtsenburgersnoff stared at Karl and in a very icy voice said, "You are wrong, and as punishment for your pestilence you will come up to the board and work out the sum in front of the whole class." So, Karl simply walked up to the blackboard and while Mr. Schmidtsenburgersnoff strutted around in front of the classroom, Karl wrote out the following:

$$1+2+3+4+5 +\ldots + \ldots + 98+99+100$$
$$1+100=101$$
$$2+99=101$$
$$3+98=101$$
$$\ldots$$
$$50 \text{ pairs} \times 101 = 5050$$

The laughter in the classroom erupted again. Mr. Schmidtsenburgersnoff turned to the board. At this point he was blinded by his rage and he did not see the details of what was written there. He saw only gibberish. The intolerant behaviour of one student was bad enough, but the whole class behaving as they were was too much! He turned to the class and roared, "For your intolerable behaviour I assign you all the following tasks." And he walked to the board, erased what Karl had written there and wrote up the following three tasks.

Find the sum of the first 200 whole numbers.

Find the sum of the whole numbers from 201 to 300.

Find the sum of the first 1000 whole numbers.

Can you figure these out?

This example of a story introduces a powerful strategy, often referred to as "Gauss' pairing method." As a story, it adheres to many of the general elements that all good stories have. There is a plot, there is a discernable beginning (but not a discernable end – more on this later), there is conflict, resolution of conflict (although not really – more on this later), imagery, human meaning, wonder, and humour. In addition to these general characteristics there is also the more specific element of pattern. In what follows we will attend to each of these elements in turn, discussing why they are so fundamental, how they were used in the example of the story presented above, and most importantly, how they can be used elsewhere. In discussing these elements we are informed by work on imagination, story design and literary technique (e.g. Baker & Greene, 1987; Bauer, 1993; Egan, 1986, 1997; Pellowsky, 1977).

PLOT

A plot seems like a rather obvious element of a story. In fact, it is hard to imagine a story without a plot. Our goal here is not to argue the obvious need for a plot but rather to discuss in greater detail exactly what the plot is, and how it contributes to the stories we are promoting.

What a plot *is*, is often confused with what a plot *does* (Johnson, 2000). What a plot *does* is move the listener (or the reader) through the events of a story, guiding not only their feelings, but also their thoughts. It prompts the listeners to ask questions, questions that will necessitate their constant attention to the story through to its conclusion. What a plot *is*, however, is a conscious effort on the part of the author to create a story line that will fulfil his or her purpose. In our case that purpose is to situate the rather mundane topic of summing arithmetic sequences in the context of human meaning (to humanize it if you will) and thus spark an interest in the students. However, it is not our intention to simply capture the students' attention through adventure, drama, comedy, or tragedy. We also intend to focus that attention on the mathematics contained within the story. For us the story is a means to an end, not an end unto itself. What is important is not that the students hear a story that contains mathematics but that they *engage in* the mathematics that emerges out of the story. The plot is our most powerful tool for achieving this.

To capture a student's attention in one context and then to transfer that attention to a different context is not an easy task. Anyone who has been frustrated by the loss of attention that occurs as they move from an introductory concrete activity to a more formalized (and perhaps abstract) lesson can attest to this difficulty. It is easy to mis-place and to mis-read a student's attention. Take for example the use of physical humour to capture students' attention – *as you walk into a classroom carrying the day's work you intentionally trip over an extension cord and fall in a brilliant display of physical acting accompanied by loud noises, displacement of furniture, and bits of paper and books flying everywhere.* There is no doubt that the fall attracted the students' attention. If you continue on with the 'act' continuing to bumble and fumble your way through the lesson there is also no doubt that you will keep their attention. If, however, you recover from your unfortunate entry into the classroom and proceed with your intended plan of teaching a riveting lesson on long-division, there is little doubt that the rapt attention you had during your initial calamity will wane. This is perhaps a bit dramatic, but no different in essence than the wane of attention that occurs as one attempts to move students from the enjoyable (and concrete) activity of listening to a story to working with pencil and paper.

So, what is it about these two scenarios – Gauss' story and tripping over extension chord – that make them different? Why does attention wane in the second scenario? Well, attention is a delicate thing – although it is easily captured it is not easily held. Constant stimulus (whether external or internal) is necessary. As Foghorn Leghorn says, "You have to be a magician to keep a kid's attention for more than five minutes these days!" This is perhaps a little bit too cynical, but nonetheless true in essence. The second scenario presented above, whereby some 'trick' is used to capture attention, suffers from the fatal consequence that it then tries to shift that attention to something that is not stimulating, or less stimulating. The first scenario does not suffer this same flaw. Instead it adheres to a fundamental principle – we want to capture a student's attention in the same direction in which we want to hold it (Dewey, 1913).

So, what are the implications of this principle for our plot? Although it is more difficult to capture a child's attention with mathematics than swordplay or fairytale princes, it is well worth it when it is time to hold their attention. As such, we construct the plot in such a way that the mathematics is featured prominently in the development of the story – it is not simply an *add-on* that we *add on* towards the end. This is not to say that other aspects of the plot cannot also be developed (such as character development, the ebb and flow of conflict, etc.) but these should not be featured to the exclusion of the mathematics. The story presented above stands as an example of this. It could be argued that the mathematics is on par with the characters in the story. It is part of Karl's character description (*"Although Karl Friedrich Gauss (1777-1855) would eventually grow up to be a brilliant mathematician (some would even say the greatest mathematician)"*), it is the challenge that Karl must meet (*"This was by far the most severe punishment the teacher had ever given out"*) and it is the weapon with which Karl conquers his adversary (*"The classroom erupted into laughter"*). Mathematics is always there, and always in the foreground. The plot even sets the stage for the transition from hearing (and/or seeing) mathematics to *doing* mathematics (*"For your intolerable behaviour I assign you all the following tasks"*). Thus, the plot accommodates the transition from *capturing* the students' attention to *holding* the students' attention.

To demonstrate these ideas further let us look at two very different versions of the same story – the story of Archimedes' death.

Version 1

> Archimedes was not only a great mathematician, he was also a great engineer. In particular, he was very good at designing 'engines of war' – that is, machines that could be used in battle. He was so good at it, in fact, that it can be said that when Marcellus' Roman army attacked Syracuse Archimedes alone held the advancing Roman army at bay. The 'engines of war' that Archimedes had designed thwarted Marcellus' Roman army at every turn. So effective were these 'engines' that even Marcellus held Archimedes in high regard. So, when Syracuse finally fell to the Roman army Marcellus gave the order that Archimedes was to be captured ... but not harmed. The soldier who eventually found Archimedes, however, did not heed these instructions. Incensed by Archimedes' refusal to abandon his work and follow him to Marcellus, the Roman soldier killed Archimedes on the spot.

This version, despite adhering to the facts of the events, puts Archimedes the man at the foreground. If properly developed, this telling could move a listener to appreciate the sheer genius of Archimedes. Unfortunately, such a telling does not deal with mathematics at the level we intend to foster in this book. So, let us now look at a second telling of the same story.

Version 2

> *It can be said that Archimedes alone held the advancing Roman army at bay. Through his brilliance he had managed to construct 'engines of war' that had frustrated Marcellus' army for weeks. The source of this brilliance, some would say, was due to Archimedes' deep and unwavering concentration. If a problem interested him he could, and would, focus on that problem to the exclusion (even neglect) of all other issues, no matter how pressing. This neglect had of course led to the 'great bath the mathematician' fiasco only a few years earlier (See chapter 5). Ultimately, this deep concentration would be both his greatest advantage and his greatest disadvantage.*
>
> *When the Roman army finally broke through Syracuse's defences, Marcellus gave the order that Archimedes was to be brought before him – alive! This order, however, as clear as it was, was not enough to quell the outrage of the soldier who eventually found Archimedes. Had the soldier known about Archimedes' habit of slipping into moments of deep thought even at inappropriate times he would not have been as enraged by Archimedes' response to his advance. "Noli turbare circulos meos" ("Do not disturb my circles"), Archimedes yelled at him. Perhaps Archimedes was unaware that this was a Roman soldier approaching. Perhaps he was even unaware that Syracuse had been overrun by the attacking army. At that moment, the only thing that Archimedes was aware of was the problem that so firmly held his attention. It is said, that even as the soldier ran Archimedes through with a spear, Archimedes never took his eyes off his diagram.*

In this telling the focus of the plot is not on Archimedes. Instead, it is on Archimedes' thought process – on his deep concentration when trying to solve a problem. This may not seem like a mathematical topic, per se, but when one considers this in the context of what students need in order to succeed in problem solving it suddenly seems to be very relevant to mathematics.

So, what differentiates the second version of this story of Archimedes' death from the first version? It is not the factual details. Both versions tell the same details: Marcellus is the leader of the Roman army. The Roman army is attacking Syracuse. Syracuse is being defended by the use of 'engines of war' designed by Archimedes. When Syracuse fell Marcellus ordered the capture of Archimedes. Archimedes was eventually killed by a Roman soldier because he rebuffed the soldier's commands.

CHAPTER 2

The difference lies in the way the plot moves the reader to experience the story. The plot, in each version, has been designed to move the reader's attention to different features of the story. In the first version that feature is Archimedes the man. In the second version that feature is Archimedes' ability to focus his mind. Although it is the plot that achieves this focusing of the listener's attention, it is us, the authors of the story, who orchestrate this focusing through the way we design it. That is, to the hearer the plot is the thread that leads them; to the writer or storyteller the plot is the weaving of that thread.

CONFLICT

Consider how young children linguistically grasp the phenomenal world around them. In dealing with temperature, they first learn 'hot' and 'cold', where 'hot' means "hotter than my body's temperature" and 'cold' means "colder than my body's temperature." These are the terms for one of the first, and most general, discriminations children make and learn to label. We recognize problems using this universal categorizing tool – good/bad, high/low, earth/sky, courage/cowardice, wet/dry, big/little, sharp/blunt, fast/slow, bitter/sweet and so endlessly on. It is as though we first have to divide things into oppositions in order to get an initial grasp on them. Holding onto such oppositions instead of recognizing the inherently complex nature of the world around us can be problematic (after all, the world is not black and white), but it can also be very useful. Somehow this initial binary classification helps us to orient our thoughts, to gain position, and to gain perspective on issues.

At a very young age (3 or 4), long before we are aware of the subtleties and nuances that life will require us to be sensitive to, we begin to sort through the daily happenings through a lens of binary opposites. Those who study young children will recognize how common such binary thinking is – the "manner in which [children] can bring some order into [their] world [is] by dividing everything into opposites" (Bettelheim, 1976, p. 74). As children get older, they come to understand that not every stranger is to be feared and that people are not all good or all bad, but they never lose this initial appreciation for binary classification.

So, how does this idea of binary classification schemes and the reliance on binary oppositions help us in creating 'good' stories? If we reflect on the kind of fantasy-stories young children enjoy so readily, we see that they are built on relatively stark binary oppositions between security/danger, good/bad, courage/cowardice, and so on. The fairy tales and stories we read to children do not create these perceptions; they capitalize on them. Story writers have long known the power of this literary tool of creating conflict through good versus evil, children versus adults, cats versus dogs, beauty versus hideousness, innocence versus corruption, and so on. From the cowboy in the white hat to the damsel in distress the inevitable struggle against their binary opposite forms the basis of popular fiction. But the idea of binary opposition is more than just clever marketing. It succeeds because we have a propensity for appreciating such conflicts. It would be imprudent, then, to ignore this powerful literary tool when creating stories for the purpose of conveying mathematics.

It is not enough, however, to simply announce that there is conflict. The conflict needs to be constructed in the course of the plot through the careful selection of opposing characters. In our example at the beginning of this chapter the main conflict is between Karl and Mr. Schmidtsenburgersnoff. There are several binary opposites that were used first to construct this conflict and then to amplify it – Karl is young while Mr. Schmidtsenburgersnoff is old; Karl is clever while Mr. Schmidtsenburgersnoff is not, Karl is jovial while Mr. Schmidtsenburgersnoff is serious, Karl is mischievous while Mr. Schmidtsenburgersnoff is strict. Each of these opposite character traits serves not only to create the conflict, but also to align the listener's allegiance with Karl. That is, the opposing qualities we choose to highlight serve not only to construct the conflict, but to orientate the listener's feelings.

To further accentuate this point we return to our hero from the previous section, Archimedes. Only this time the context is different.

There was a time in Archimedes' life when he turned his attention to the wonders of the circle. Archimedes knew that there existed a special relationship between the distance around the circle and the distance across the circle, that is, between the circumference of a circle and its diameter. And he spent long hours trying to figure out exactly what this relationship was.[*]

As advanced as the Egyptians were, they had never seemed to come up with a very good way to measure a circle. They would construct a cylinder of the same circumference and then measure how much rope it took to wrap around it. This method was still in use in Archimedes' time. In fact, it was the preferred method of one of Archimedes' good friends Bartholomew. Bartholomew was well known throughout Syracuse as one of the best circle measurers in town and Archimedes often went to him when he had a particularly difficult circle to measure. But you could imagine that with such a good reputation for precision and such a high demand for circle measurement that Bartholomew was falling behind on his commitments. As a result, Archimedes needed to start measuring his own circles.

Bartholomew laughed at his old friend when he heard of Archimedes' plans to measure his own circles. After all, it was well known that Archimedes preferred to work with pencil and paper rather than with hammer and chisel. Nonetheless, he set about trying to come up with a better method to measure the circumference of a circle. It is not clear in what circumstances Archimedes came up with his idea, although it is almost certain that it did

---

[*] We return to this story and this special relationship in Chapter 5.

CHAPTER 2

not include a bath or any nudity[*]*, but an idea eventually came to him. Archimedes realized that if he drew a square inside his circle (not just any square, mind you, the biggest square possible with its corners touching the circle) as well as a square outside his circle (the smallest square possible with its sides touching the circle) then the circumference of the circle would be somewhere between the perimeter of the two squares. This was easy enough to do, but it generated too large a set of possibilities for the circumference of the circle. So, he switched to drawing polygons with more sides – pentagons, then hexagons, and so on. By the time he got up to twelve sided polygons, he found that he was producing answers as accurate as his friend Bartholomew. Bartholomew didn't laugh anymore. He eventually went out of business and had to take early retirement. He moved to Jamaica where he spent his time fishing and making wooden circles for the tourists.*

Okay, we never said that our stories had to be historically accurate. We trust that students would be able to distinguish historical detail from humorous intermezzo. Getting back to our story, the casting of the relatively onerous and clumsy way of measuring circles as exemplified by Bartholomew versus the elegance of Archimedes' solution sets up a nice conflict, not between Archimedes and Bartholomew, but between the theoretical and the practical. By accentuating Bartholomew's clumsiness and Archimedes' elegance the listener's allegiance is drawn towards Archimedes. In so doing, the elegance and the power of Archimedes' theoretical approach to measuring circles is more easily appreciated. This is no small feat considering that for an elementary school student the most obvious (and often practiced) way of measuring a circle is to lay a string around its perimeter and then to measure the outstretched string. This method is no different than that of Bartholomew.

This brings up another point regarding the selection and construction of characters through whom the conflict arises. In the introductory story of this chapter the characters are constructed so as to help listeners *align* themselves with Karl. This differs from saying that the listener's feelings are oriented towards Karl. Up until now we have only talked about orienting feelings or building allegiances. Alignment is slightly different. It has more to do with who the listener can relate to rather than who they are 'cheering' for. In the story of Karl everything from his age to the setting of a classroom has been designed to help the listener relate to Karl. In the most recent story of Archimedes and Bartholomew the story has been written, although to much lesser extent, to help the listener relate to Bartholomew. Here is a character who is hard working and has a very practical method of measuring circles that is not too dissimilar from the method that the listener may be familiar with. The hope is that the listener will align themselves with Bartholomew and then be moved to improve upon their own thinking when presented with Archimedes alternate method. Although this is sometimes difficult to do there is one very

---

[*] This story is revisited in Chapter 5.

important rule that needs to be followed to guard against failure – never vilify the character that you want the listeners to align themselves with. This is why Bartholomew is not portrayed as Archimedes' nemesis.

Once a conflict is created it seems only natural to expect that this conflict then be resolved. In the story of Gauss this is both true and false. It is true that the initial conflict between Karl and Mr. Schmidtsenburgersnoff is resolved with Karl getting the better of his foe. However, this is followed up with a new conflict – a conflict between Mr. Schmidtsenburgersnoff and the entire class. This is no accident. The conclusion of the story with an unresolved conflict is a deliberate strategy for facilitating the transition from listening to doing. This strategy is further enhanced if the final conflict can be constructed so as to help the listener align themselves with the protagonist of the story. In this case the protagonist becomes all of the students in Karl's class. The alignment here is obvious – the class of students who are listening to the story will easily relate themselves to the class of students in the story. In a way, the story introduces a mathematical activity and then intertwines with this activity. This issue is discussed in detail in Chapter 5.

IMAGES

One result of the development of language was the discovery that words can be used to evoke images in the minds of their hearers, and that these images can have as powerful emotional effects as reality might, and in some cases even more.

Images created in traditional oral cultures have the crucial social role of aiding memorization. So we find myths replete with vivid and often bizarre images that give them what we might categorize as powerful literary impact. The original purpose of this 'literary impact' was the urgent need to preserve knowledge in cultures without writing. They achieved this by stimulating a range of psychological effects, which continue today in quite different circumstances, long outliving the social purpose they were developed for. Similarly, language development in children leads to the capacity to evoke mental images of what is not present and to feel about them as though they were real. Recall, as most of us can quite vividly, images from some of the earliest stories you remember. Some images, no doubt, are influenced by pictures in books, but it is common to find that the most vivid and evocative images are those we generate for ourselves while listening to stories (Egan, 1986).

There are a number of techniques for systematically using images in teaching. One such technique, called *Guided Imagery*, involves the teacher taking the students verbally to some different time and place by describing the sights, sounds, and smells of this other time and place. *Guided Imagery* can be a powerfully effective technique in many circumstances. What we mean by the use of images here, however, is on a much smaller scale. It does not require relatively elaborate preparations or set-piece performances. Rather it requires the teacher to be more consistently conscious of the array of vivid images that are a part of every topic and to draw on them consistently in vivifying knowledge and concepts.

CHAPTER 2

In the context of mathematics, images are almost completely useless as a vehicle for transmission of content. But as a vehicle for capturing the imagination of listeners it is an indispensable tool. In many ways the images used are is what makes the story worth listening to. Without them what is said may become a boring and loosely connected string of facts. The seemingly meaningless details that are woven into the fabric of the story add colour and drama. In the story of Karl, images were used to add detail to the story. The descriptions of the school and Karl's unique way of tormenting his teacher, although marginally relevant to the plot, are details added to make the story more palatable. It would have been sufficient to say that Karl was mischievous and at the time was behaving badly. The added details about the nature of his misbehaviour give personality to the characters as well as add humour to the situation. Together they combine to make the story more enjoyable and more memorable.

HUMAN MEANING

Scientific knowledge, especially as stacked in textbooks, has an aura of objectivity – it is secure, uninfluenced by what we might hope or fear, and a solid assertion of what is true. Or, at least, that is what we are supposed to think. Knowledge, once formed, tends to become disembodied from its human origins. That is, while knowledge is preserved in the form of books, formulas, proofs, theorems, and such, we must not forget that before all this the formation of knowledge was the result of human thought, effort, and desire. Knowledge is a product of human hopes and fears; our emotions are crucial to its development, and its meaning cannot be truly understood if seen as some bloodless and emotionless enterprise.

Text-books, in particular mathematics textbooks, have tended to disguise from us the simple truth that all knowledge is human knowledge. Too often textbook writers seem to forget this, and science and mathematics texts seem particularly 'inhuman'. This is especially true when considering that human emotions provide one of the easiest tools that students have available for understanding the material in texts. The educational trick is to display knowledge as the product of human ingenuity, energy, passion, hope, fear, and so on. People not too dissimilar from ourselves made it, invented it, discovered it, and formulated it for human purposes, and they did so with human motives. Instead of representing knowledge as a given – telling students the rules for the use of parentheses or for solving equations and giving them exercises until they get the rules right – we might make the knowledge memorable and meaningful by re-embedding it in the context of its original invention or human uses. This might be dramatically shown in mathematics. When students learn a mathematical relation by seeing who invented it and for what purpose, it is more easily learned, more clearly understood, and more likely remembered. The 'who' can be a single person (Karl Friedrich Gauss), a culture (ancient Greeks), or imaginary characters.

So while teaching mathematics we might sensibly remember that everything we teach has a human source – the decimal point and quadratic equations were invented by someone – and that by bringing to the fore the human emotions, ambitions, intentions, fears, and so on, we can expect to engage our students' imaginations in learning. The story of Karl is a perfect example of this. Although the historical truth of this story can be argued (especially given the creative liberties we have taken), what cannot be argued is the human element that is built into the story. We have already talked about the ability of this story to align the listeners first with Karl's character and then with Karl's classmates. The method for adding sequences of numbers that Gauss developed is presented, not as an abstract and disconnected algorithm, but as a method that grew out of a human need and personalized ingenuity. The algorithm has a human context, and as such takes on greater human meaning. Students can relate to Karl and his plight, they can appreciate his situation, and they can share in his accomplishment. In constructing the story in this way we are, in essence, constructing human meaning.

As a completely different example consider the renowned theorem of Pythagoras. If high school graduates remember only one theorem from their mathematical experience, it would most likely be this one. Through some method of repeated application the name for this one formula has stuck in their minds. What may not have stuck, however, are the details of the relationship ($a^2 + b^2 = c^2$) or where it is appropriate to use it to calculate a third side of a triangle when given the first two. What is missing for these graduates is a human connection to the theorem. For them 'Pythagoras' was something to be memorized and to be used in exercises dealing with abstract situations. If, perhaps, they had seen the great human need for constructing right angles that this relationship satisfied they would likely have a greater connection to the theorem. By tying knots at equal distances in a rope, or making triangles with sticks of different integer lengths measured by the same unit, the ancient engineers and carpenters noticed that only a few configurations result in right angles. Students can relive this experience and discover for themselves a few such configurations, nowadays referred to as Pythagorean triples.

Both of these examples – Gauss and Pythagoras – have something in common: they construct human meaning in the third person. That is, we can write (and have written) the stories so that the listener will see that the mathematics had meaning to some human at some time, even if that person and/or time are fictional. A more powerful way to create human meaning in mathematics is through the first person. That is, to make the mathematics meaningful to the listeners, and to have them engage in the mathematics themselves. This is not to say that every time someone is asked to 'do' some mathematics they will find deeply personal meaning in the act. What it does say, however, is that if they do not 'do' mathematics they will definitely not find personal meaning in it. As such, the orchestration of first person human meaning will necessitate a transition from listening to mathematics in the story to doing the mathematics in the story. As mentioned earlier, the story of Karl facilitates a move in this direction through the invitation to the class to participate in the conclusion of the story. This is discussed further in Chapter 8, Stories that ask a question, and Chapter 12, Using existing stories.

CHAPTER 2

THE SENSE OF WONDER

It is easy to feel the emotion of wonder in the face of the dramatic features of the natural world – a mountain view, a gold and scarlet sunset, a vast waterfall, and the immensity of space. Wonder is a kind of emotional memory of what we have lost. The "overflow of powerful feelings" that accompanies wonder can, like the associations discussed above, be directed to almost any object. Everything we see around us can be re-seen in the light of wonder. Wonder can be an engine of intellectual inquiry. It is a part of literate rationality's persistent questioning.

There are many nuances to the term wonder. First and foremost is the act of wondering, that can become a pivot for mathematical instruction. To engage students in mathematics is to ignite the fires of curiosity, to get them wondering why things are as they are. "I wonder why…" is the beginning of scientific thinking. Nature becomes an object of wonder and inquiry. I wonder why the bathwater rises as I sink into it? I wonder how many worms there are in the garden? I wonder why the sky is blue? I wonder how many times is it possible to cut a string in half? A very direct way to get students to wonder about things in mathematics is to ask them 'why' something is as it is. Why do we need to have a zero? Why is $\pi = 3.14$ (or is it)? Why is 1 not a prime number? Why does column addition work? The answers to each of these questions, when explored and discovered by students, will lead to a greater understanding of mathematics.

There is a second, and equally powerful, meaning to the word wonder. This usage is to instil wonder, to be in awe of something, or to see it as wonderful. Stimulating wonder energizes the imagination. In our teaching of mathematics, then, we will be sensible to attend to how one can evoke a sense of wonder in relation to the topic we are dealing with. This will require the teacher to reflect on the topic and locate what is wonderful within it. Anything, seen in the right light, can be seen as wonderful. Even if we are learning how to deal with the everyday transactions of shopping, one can evoke some sense of wonder by embedding the task in a context that draws attention to the astonishing variety of goods brought from all corners of the world, the ingenuity that has gone into arranging food in hygienic containers with stunning efficiency, the UPC codes by which products are recognized, the work of generations of chemists and physicists that has gone into making such taken-for-granted products as toothpaste and other cleaners, fruit juices, frozen peas, and so on. This does not demand lengthy factual lessons on the background of each item, but rather a constant alertness to the wonders of the things around us. Unfortunately, it is hard for some people to pull back from their utilitarian routines. However, the task of stimulating interest in mathematics often involves locating mathematics in the wider context of wonder, and, of course, in being alert to the students' recognition of wonder. A part of good teaching that helps the transition to a richer understanding of mathematics is locating something wonderful in everything we teach; doing so will not only make learning easier for the student, but will also be more interesting and satisfying for the teacher.

Oh sure, one may ask, as students surely will, what is there about mathematics that is so awe inspiring as to elevate its status to that of wonder when, for the most part, mathematical topics traditionally encountered in school are taken for granted and do not offer much to wonder about. There is no answer to such a challenge. For like beauty, wonder is in the eye of the beholder. We can only say that for many, ourselves included, there is wonder in everything in mathematics. From numbers to shapes to algorithms the tightly knit web of connections that supports what we call mathematics is awe-inspiring. At every turn and in everything we do in relation to mathematics we are reminded of the connections that binds it together into a cohesive whole. However, we do not expect our students to experience the same feelings of wonder that we do. They have not seen enough of mathematics to stand in awe of its grandeur. Our goals for our students are much more modest. We want them to see the wonder in individual mathematical concepts. If wonder is an engine of enquiry, then teachers must find a way to stimulate and use learners' sense of wonder to help them wonder about things they learn or observe, and in so doing re-see things as wonderful.

Consider, yet again, our introductory story about Karl. With an appropriate pause in the telling technique – to be explored in Chapter 3 – students may wonder about how Karl could complete the seemingly impossible task imposed by the teacher. It is possible to turn the problem to the class before revealing the solution. Personal attempts to attack the problem may foster appreciation of the ingenuity of the Gauss' pairing method. Further, though there is nothing in the story that can be explicitly identified by a student as wonderful there are many implicit things that, with the help of the teacher, can be brought to the attention of the student. To begin with, the algorithm that Karl presents is highly flexible. Not only can it assist in adding up very large sequences of numbers (or sequences of very large numbers) it can also work on a large variety of sequences. Arithmetic sequences of multiples such as 3, 6, 9, ... can just as efficiently be solved as sequences of non-multiples such as 2, 5, 8, ... Decreasing sequences can be added as easily as increasing sequences and sequences involving both positive and negative numbers. The algorithm allows students to feel (perhaps for the first time) the power of control that they can have over a large number of situations with a relatively small collection of tools.

Besides flexibility, Gauss' pairing method for determining the sum of the sequence has great utility. It allows a student who holds its secrets to be able to solve a great number of problems. From stacks of soup cans in the grocery store to the great pyramids of the ancient world the algorithm enables them to calculate quickly how many objects (soup cans, blocks of stones) there are in these geometric constructs. Like the flexibility of the algorithm, the utility of the algorithm is something that is implicit within the story. It takes the teacher to bring them alive.

HUMOR

Humour, like imagery, can be used to make a story more palatable. It can colour our stories with details and engage our students' emotions in a way that mathematics typically does not. Depending on how it is used, humour can capture attention or focus attention. It can provide an access point for some students as well as an outlet for others. Through humorous anecdotes, comical characters, or laughable situations, humour can both ignite and delight the mind. We suggest that humour can be used as part of telling a story.

Humour, most simply described, is the incongruence between what is expected and what occurs. This definition can be used to describe a multitude of various uses of humour in our stories. From the silliness of Karl's misbehaviours to the outrageous retirement destination of Bartholomew, the seemingly useless details add colour to our stories. Primary school students, in particular, appreciate silly antics. Why not insert them into the story? Introduce a hilarious noise that is made every time a specific character sits, walks, blinks, sneezes ... whatever. But better than describing it, imitate it – add a soundtrack to a story and the children will be engaged. For the more mature students a twist on the expected is a better bet. Introduce completely incongruent elements into the story – Eratosthenes has a cell phone, Archimedes has a pet buffalo, Gauss' favourite number is 147. Such seemingly frivolous details will make the students sit up and take notice. We added humorous detail in several stories discussed in this chapter. Recall Karl's favourite trick of imitating the sound of creaking wood, recall the place of retirement for Bartholomew.

A more difficult task is to integrate humour in such a way that it focuses attention on mathematics. The example above about Gauss' favourite number can achieve this. Upon hearing that it is 147 students will immediately ask why – what is it about this number that is so special? This is now an optimum situation for teaching. Attention has been focused on mathematics through a simple trick of incongruence.

PATTERNS

> *When I read a math paper, it's no different than a musician reading a score. In each case the pleasure comes from the play of patterns, the harmonies and contrasts.* (Rudy Rucker, 1999, p. 11)

Many have argued that mathematics is the science of patterns. At the same time, research has repeatedly shown that children have a seemingly natural disposition towards patterns and patterning activity. It makes sense then that we should want to make use of this very powerful tool in the teaching of mathematics. According to Mason (1996), patterns are the 'heart and soul' of mathematics and, as such, many mathematical activities can be structured around attending to patterns. Patterns have the power to engage students, to embody mathematics, and to activate imaginations. In fact, some of the important roles of patterns are similar to those of stories – they can be used to introduce concepts or activities, they can be used to explain mathematical ideas that learners find difficult, they can be used to ask a question, and they can be used to instil wonder. Ultimately, the question is not where can we use patterns in the teaching of mathematics, but where can we not?

Consider the story of Karl from the beginning of this chapter. The solution that Karl suggested involved a pattern. The challenge that was eventually set for the rest of the class can be resolved involving a pattern, or at least this is the intention. In fact, the means to solving the tasks set for the rest of the class lie in the recognition of the analogy that exists between the various questions and the solution strategy that Gauss came up with. The story of Archimedes and circle measurement can be developed to an activity of pattern recognition and serve to access a variety of different topics from ideas on convergence to the relationship between the circumference of a circle and its radius. We elaborate on this in Chapter 5.

SUMMARY

In this chapter we presented several stories that can be told in a mathematics classroom and discussed the elements that make these stories interesting, memorable and engaging. We considered these components as means towards the goal of students learning mathematics through engaging in a meaningful activity.

CHAPTER 3

STORYTELLING

The art of telling a story – when the teller has found the story to his mind – has been written on by many, and I hope I shall offend none when I say that the writers of these books fail for this reason – they attempt the impossible. (Burrell, 1926, p. 3)

Telling a story resembles telling a joke. The intention can be lost if told inappropriately. The text that makes us laugh may also make us shrug and wonder how someone thought this was funny. Telling is an art, an act of improvisation.

Storytelling is believed to be one of the oldest forms of human art and also the "first conscious form of literary communication" (Shedlock, 1924, p.xiii). Burrel (1926) referred to storytelling as "Nature's way of teaching" (p. 2). It is "older than history and is not bounded by one civilization, one continent, or one race" (Baker and Greene, 1987, p.1). The idea of universality and timelessness of storytelling has been described by Burrell (1926) as "an event so usual that no latitude and no century can have been without it" (p. 5). Storytelling developed in early civilizations as it satisfied the need of humans to communicate with other humans, the need to entertain and self-entertain, and the need to explain the physical world. Furthermore, storytelling developed as it fulfilled the aesthetic need for artistic expression and the desire to record events or actions of ancestors (Pellowski, 1977).

Baker and Greene (1987) follow Lewis Carroll, who calls stories 'love gifts' and extend this metaphor to the telling of a story, which they refer to as 'giving a gift'. Having interviewed hundreds of tellers, casual and professional, Haven (2000) proposed the following definition:

STORYTELLING: The art of using language, vocalization, and/or physical movement and gesture to reveal the elements and images of a story to a specific, live audience (p. 215)

Haven further noted that "storytelling is both the most basic mode of human communication and a powerful performance art form" (p. 216). Luckily, most teachers are masters of this art. They know how to make students interested in a story and how to change the story to accommodate the audience. However, very few bring this talent to a mathematics classroom.

STORYTELLING BY STORYTELLERS

There are professional storytellers. Even though there are no departments of storytelling at colleges and universities and no professors of storytelling, there are

CHAPTER 3

individuals for whom storytelling is their occupation. They make their living from it. They tell stories on stage, at parks and bookstores, at coffee houses and concert halls, at professional gatherings and museums, at churches and temples, in libraries and hospitals, at birthday parties and county fairs, at festivals or at any special event where people may gather. There are annual storytelling events in public libraries and there is a National Association for the Preservation and Perpetuation of Storytelling (NAPPS).

Some storytellers are professional actors, some are amateurs. There are, however, important differences between acting and storytelling, the main of which is the relationship with the audience. For a storyteller the audience is alive and not unseen in a darkened hall, and unlike the actor on a stage, who follows a practiced script, a storyteller changes the script based on a feedback from the audience.

Many guides have been written by and for professional storytellers (e.g., Baker & Greene, 1987; Bauer, 1993; Burrell, 1971; Shedlock, 1924) that inform storytellers' choices of what to tell and how to tell, what elements to attend to in choosing a good story for any specific occasion. These guides provide plenty of resources for good stories that are known to appeal to audiences of different age groups and for different purposes. They also explain what artifacts (puppets, decorations, exhibits, masks, posters, crafts, pictures, etc.) may be used to accompany a story, when to raise voice and when to slow down, when to pause, what gestures to make or not to make, and even how to breathe, how to arrange furniture and what to wear. They warn the tellers of common pitfalls, such as the use of words unfamiliar to the audience or lowering the standard via over-explanation or over-illustration (Shedlock, 1924). There is also professional help on how to get started, how to choose a site, how to enhance storytelling performance with riddles, songs, games or magic tricks. Moreover, professionals offer helpful advice on what do when one gets bored with a specific story, or when one gets nervous in front of the audience, and even some hints on how to deal with discipline or interruption during storytelling.

Though learning from master storytellers' tricks of the trade is helpful for those who only occasionally engage in storytelling, we turn in this chapter to a more specific context – storytelling in a mathematics classroom. However, before we proceed to the special case on mathematics, we turn to storytelling in a classroom, or any educational setting in general.

STORYTELLING IN EDUCATIONAL CONTEXT

The joyful experience of an audience in listening to good stories told well may be a good enough reason for professional storytellers to keep telling stories. Among many psychological and educational benefits of storytelling, "the dramatic joy we bring to children and to ourselves" was considered by Baker and Greene (1987) as "the best reason of all" (p. 25).

However, teachers are interested not only in a story itself and its dramatic appeal and amusement to listeners. They are mostly interested in telling a story as a means to another end. Stories are told to raise interest and make listeners think. In more general terms, Baker and Greene (1987) suggest that storytelling has a positive effect on a child's cognitive and social development. They highlight the significance of stories for educators who fear that schools' emphasis on cognitive skills may be at the expense of children's affective development. They exemplify how storytelling "gives children insight into the motives and patterns of human behaviour" (p. 22) and help children overcome psychological problems.

Haven (2000) summarized 10 benefits of storytelling as an educational tool:

1. Storytelling is a powerful and effective element in an effort to improve and develop all four primary language arts skills (reading, writing, listening and speaking).
2. Information (both concepts and facts) is remembered better and longer when presented in story form.
3. Storytelling is a powerful and effective interdisciplinary, cross-curriculum teaching tool.
4. Storytelling positively motivates students to learn. Told stories focus student attention and learning and excite students to pursue related studies.
5. Storytelling effectively builds student self-confidence and self-esteem.
6. Storytelling effectively engages and develops the skills of imagination and creativity better than any other single classroom activity.
7. Storytelling engages and entertains.
8. Storytelling creates empathy and sense of connectedness.
9. Storytelling improves analytical and problem –solving skills
10. Storytelling creates valuable links to community and heritage.

It is not surprising that the first benefit mentioned takes the lion's share of attention in literature. Looking through books identified by a 'storytelling' subject descriptor in a library, we noticed that about three quarters of these books specifically attend to various forms of language arts. There appears to be a natural connection between telling stories and development of literacy, extension of vocabulary, introduction to patterns of language, and improvement of both oral and written language skills. The story form is considered the foundation of how we understand and conceptualise language (Haven, 2000).

The tenth, the last benefit mentioned, has become extremely popular in recent years, at least in Canada, with enforced educational emphasis on multiculturalism and First Nations. Storytelling serves as the means to introduce children to different traditions and civilizations and keep the cultural heritage of different peoples alive.

Most writers agree that storytelling can support curriculum. However, among their specific examples of what can lend support to curriculum, we find very little mention of Mathematics. We find this unfortunate and attempt to fill this gap.

CHAPTER 3

STORYTELLING IN THE MATHEMATICS CLASSROOM

Stories are not popular in mathematics classrooms. Most mathematics classroom instruction consists of short explanations by the teacher followed by a series of examples that students then imitate in their own work. Even when advanced mathematical thinking or problem solving is involved, it is seldom accompanied by a story. Even though many writers mention storytelling as 'cross-curriculum tool', their examples 'cross' language arts with history or science, but conveniently do not involve mathematics.

So, what is the benefit, if any, of bringing storytelling into a mathematics classroom? In addition to all the benefits mentioned in the previous section, and especially support for memory (2), motivation (4), engagement (7), and improvement of analytical skills (9), Mathematics stories have additional purposes. They can introduce or explain hard concepts in a memorable fashion and involve students in mathematical activity. They can bring a human element to a subject that is too often perceived as dry and technical. They can bring to the mathematics classroom unexpected novelty and a change of activity. They can refresh and support the creative atmosphere and provide entertainment. And even though entertainment is rarely mentioned as a goal in an educational context, its value in supporting a productive learning environment should not be overlooked.

"The secret of story-telling cannot be put on paper" (Burrell, 1926/1971, p. 51). The secret is in feeling the audience, engaging the audience, and varying the script where necessary. As such, in what follows we engage in a dangerous attempt. It is an attempt to exemplify on paper what we believe *telling* a story is about. We count here on the reader's imagination to bring 'colour' and 'flavour' to the text and introduce tone changes, pauses, emphases on specific words or phrases, or moments of silence.

THE FARMER AND THE CROW: TELLING OF A STORY

Consider the following story (Egan, 1986, p. 79), often used to exemplify number sense and the development of the human ability to count. We first present a popular story and then illustrate how it can be told in order to achieve its full potential power.

> *[This is] the story of the crow that was eating a farmer's grain. The farmer decided to shoot the crow. It had made its nest in his barn. But whenever the farmer approached the barn, the crow flew away. When he left the barn, the crow flew back. Thinking to trick the crow, the farmer took a friend with him to the barn. The farmer stayed in the barn when the friend left. But the crow was not fooled, and stayed in his tree until the farmer came out too. The next day the farmer took two friends with him to the barn, and he stayed behind when the two friends left. But still the crow waited till he came out before returning to its nest. The next day the farmer took three friends, with the same result. Next he took four, and then five friends. When*

the five came out, the farmer remaining behind, the crow flew back to its nest, and the farmer shot it.

Consider the following variation on the crow story. The plot remains the same. What changes is the way the story is presented to the audience. Let us *tell* the story.

"Once upon a time, in a land far away from here, there lived a farmer. He worked hard on the fields to provide for his family. After the harvest, he put his grain in a small barn that he built beside his field. What was his name? Let's give him a name. [Turning to one of the students] What do you want to call this farmer?"

"Travis"

"Travis? Have you ever met a farmer named Travis?"

"Jake"

"Which name do you want? OK, Jake. So this is a story about farmer Jake and a crow. Why a crow? I'll tell you why. There was an ugly crow that made its nest in the barn. Worst of all, this crow was eating Jake's grain. So Jake decided to shoot the crow. What would you do if someone was eating the grain that you had grown to feed your family? Oh – I see. You do not like shooting. OK. I'm with you. I'm changing the story. The farmer decided to get rid of the crow peacefully, to capture him. But whenever the farmer approached the barn, the crow flew away. How can I catch the crow? – thought Jake."

Here we can stop and have students make several suggestions. For some suggestions a teacher's response can be: "In fact, Jake tried this, but it didn't work. So he needed to try something different." And then the telling continues.

"So Jake thought and thought and thought, and then **suddenly**, he had an idea."
The bold word above suggest an emphasis in a tone of the teller.

"He decided to bring a friend with him to the barn. What was the friend's name?"

"George."

"So one day farmer Jake and his friend George went to the barn together. After a while George left and farmer Jake stayed behind and waited for the crow. But [pause], the crow didn't come back. The crow was not fooled; he stayed away until the farmer left the barn. Jake was disappointed and tired. He had waited for many hours in the barn and the crow had not come back; the crow had seen through Jake's plan. So, again, Jake thought and thought and thought and then **suddenly**..."
Pause here, let a student continue. If a spontaneous answer doesn't appear within seconds, it can be provoked with a question, like "Do you know what happened?"

"He had another idea?"

"Exactly. And do you know what this idea was? No? He decided to bring two friends with him to the barn. So Jake and George invited – who?"

"Joe?"

"Invited Joe to join them. The next morning farmer Jake and his friends George and Joe went together to the barn. [To a student] – Can you continue telling the story?"

"George and Joe left, Jake stayed and the crow did not return".

CHAPTER 3

"Please *tell* us the *story*, don't just summarize the facts."

"Jake, George and Joe went together to the barn. It was a nice morning and they enjoyed their leisurely stroll. After a while George and Joe left and farmer Jake stayed and waited for the crow to return. But [pause], the crow didn't come back. The crow was not fooled; it stayed away from the barn until the farmer left. Jake was very disappointed. And again he was very tired from waiting for hours in barn for the crow to come back. So he thought and thought and thought ..."

"Great. Thanks. Who can continue the story?"

At this stage the students can take turns, encouraged to fill in the details
[...]

"So the next day the farmer Jake and his good friends George and Joe, their wives Emily and Francheska, and Emily's sister Mary went to the barn. George and Joe, their wives Emily and Francheska, and Emily's sister Mary left, while Jake stayed and waited for the crow. But [pause]."

"Here I must interrupt and tell you exactly what happened that day. If some of you felt that our story was getting repetitive and boring, pay attention here. As we know, farmer Jake stayed and waited for the crow. He waited and waited and waited, and ... the crow did come back. And finally, Jake was able to get rid of the crow, peacefully of course. [To a student] You look surprised. But that's where our story ends. What happened to the farmer? He lived happily ever after and he sent his friends George and Joe, their wives Emily and Francheska, and Emily's sister Mary 'Thank You' cards. Or maybe he had a great feast and invited them over. You tell me. And the crow never bothered him again. And even if he did, Jake would have known how to get rid of it. Peacefully, of course. And they lived happily ever after. So that's our story for today. By the way, what is this story about?"

AFTER THE STORY IS TOLD

Having told the story, in order to provoke a conversation, a possible question to present to the students is "Did the crow know how to count to 4, but couldn't count up to 5 or 6? And what does it mean to know how to count? What is the essence of counting?"

In fact, several species share number sense with humans, but only humans have developed the ability to count, that is, to put number words in one-to-one correspondence with the objects being counted and to assign that last number in the sequence to the totality of objects in the set. This story may help children, and not only children, distinguish between number sense, which is innate, and counting, which is – though accessible at a very young age – a product of human ingenuity and achievement. Cave men did not count, but, with small numbers, they had the ability to distinguish between different numbers of objects. The reflection of this is found in language development. For example, in Hebrew – the most ancient language still alive – the word for 'many' (harbe) has the same root as the word for 'four' (arba). This resemblance in words echoes that once upon a time these amounts were signified similarly.

The lesson may continue with an attempt to find the limit of the human sense of quantity, that is, what numbers of objects we can recognize without actual counting. The teacher may show different number of objects for a split second. Of course, there will be no time to count, but most children will easily recognize the number when it is 4 or 5. Recognition of sets larger than 5 will most likely depend on a pattern. For example, the following picture presents 9 and 10 objects. The ease with which the number is recognized, without counting, depends on the pattern in which the objects appear.

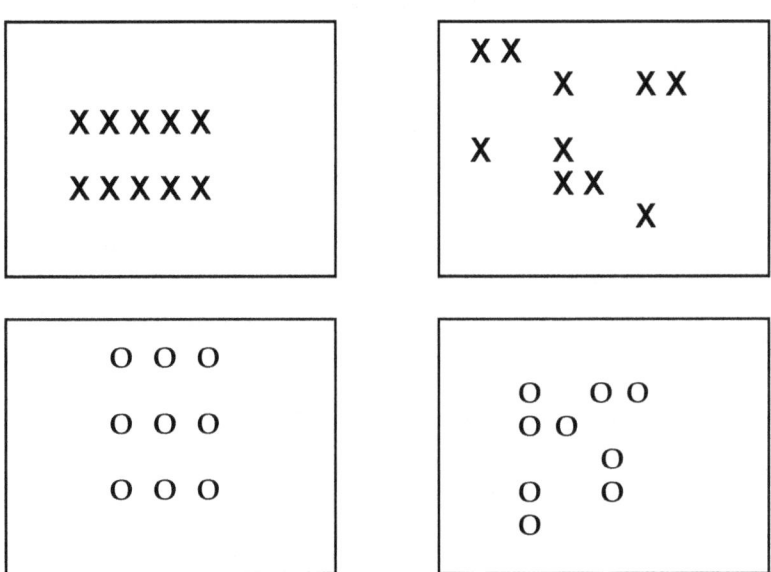

While younger students (Grades 1-2) may learn to appreciate the wonders of counting, for older students (Grade 4-5) the activity may develop into collecting data about the human sense of quantity and representing it on a bar graph.

According to Egan (1986) the crow story sets number sense and counting as 'abstract binary opposites' – a cognitive tool possessed by young learners that contributes to their engagement with the content. However, existence of 'abstract binary opposites' or any conflict in a story may be insufficient to create engagement. It is the story-teller who makes (or helps) it happen. Though nuances in the telling, such as raising the voice, changing pace or pausing, are hard to exemplify on paper, we attempted to do just that. Such nuances can be learned only by experience.

We also exemplified several ideas for student involvement in story telling. Such involvement ranges from simple answers, such as choosing names for places and characters and re-telling repetitive parts of the story to adding variety and flavour. What can be seen as temporarily getting 'off track' may, in fact, help in keeping students focused, interested and engaged.

CHAPTER 3

At times teachers who experience our stories in our classrooms seeks advice on story telling, or ask us to identify features that 'work'. We believe that advice from experienced story tellers can be helpful only to a certain degree. The best way to learn storytelling is simply to tell stories. However, we shall allow ourselves to give a few bits of advice.

Tell any story in your own words. Attempts to memorize divert attention away from the experience. If storytelling becomes part of your teaching style, find a way to announce a 'story time'. This can be a special gesture or a pose that you chose for your stories that students learn to recognize. The words 'once upon a time', recognized as a popular introduction of folk tales, may serve as a good start for any story, and may be used with humour if a story does not resemble a folk tale. Change the story as appropriate – feel the audience and involve the audience. Be flexible in accepting students' suggestions. If a story has a repetitive pattern, you may invite one of your students to tell part of the story. Try to ensure a smooth transition between the story and a subsequent discussion or activity. Collect different stories, adjust them to your purposes so that they feel like your own. And, of course, do not forget mathematics. After all, while stories serve many different purposes, social and psychological, our main purpose is to enhance the learning of mathematics.

Arthur Burrell (1926), whose quote started this chapter, made the following observation about guidelines on storytelling in his *Guide to Story Telling*: "When we have written out our few rules [...] all that is of real value has been omitted" (p. 3). As such, we invite the reader to find the 'real value' between the lines.

CHAPTER 4

STORIES THAT SET A FRAME OR A BACKGROUND

RIDDLE OF THE SPHINX

In Greek Mythology the Sphinx was a monster combining many shapes. She had the face and voice of a woman; the torso, feet and tail of a lion; the wings of a bird; and the claws of a griffin. She sat on a mountain outside of Thebes, ambushed travelers and asked riddles of all who passed by. When the traveler failed to solve her riddle, the Sphinx tore his body into pieces. The only way to destroy the Sphinx was to find a man who could solve the Sphinx's riddles. The Thebans offered sovereignty over Thebes to any man who succeeded in this. According to the legend, the greatness of the prize tempted many men to try, but they all experienced a cruel death. After many had already perished, Oedipus gave the right answer, and the Sphinx threw herself from the citadel and died. The riddle Oedipus solved was: What goes on four legs in the morning, on two legs at noon, and on three legs in the evening?[*]

By solving the Sphinx's riddle, Oedipus became the King of Thebes (and also married his own mother Queen Jocasta, but this is not of our concern here). If all this seems to be out of place in the discussion of teaching mathematics, we appreciate the reader's patience and promise that it will soon become clear. We bring forth this legend not for our love of riddles but in order to draw an analogy.

In the Riddle of the Sphinx legend the riddle itself has nothing to do with the story. That is to say, it could have been any other riddle. Though experts in mythology would suggest that the riddle that Oedipus solved was special in that it concerned the nature of man rather than nature of things, we assert that another riddle could have been embedded in the story. The riddle could have been that of a missing dollar paradox, the Towers of Hanoi, the traveling salesman or Riemann's hypothesis. The riddle could even have been a mundane textbook problem of two trains that eventually meet or two hoses that fill a pool with water. That is why we see the story line as a background or frame. Though the story and the problem are connected, they do not intertwine with one another and it is possible to separate the two. Like a photo on a different background or a painting in a different frame, the same riddle can appear within a different story. Similarly, any other problem/riddle could be presented on the background (in the frame) of the Riddle of the Sphinx myth. In fact, several computer games and video games have been created with the

---

[*] **The solution:** A man, who crawls on all fours as a baby, walks on two legs as an adult, and walks with a cane in old age. (Of course morning, noon, and night are metaphors for the stages in a man's life.)

CHAPTER 4

name Riddle of the Sphinx, in which the players, who are travelers and adventurers, have to solve different problems, presumably given by the e-Sphinx. The prize offered to the players is not a kingdom but rather the thrill of pursuit.

The Riddle of the Sphinx is the metaphor we have chosen to exemplify the difference between the story as a picture and a story as frame. We consider an additional example to highlight this distinction.

FRAME OR FOCUS?

The Tangram puzzle is a popular tool in elementary school mathematics. It can be used as a recreational activity, inviting students to make a variety of shapes of tangram pieces, and it also can be used to explore relationships among geometric shapes. Tangrams can simply be handed to students with an assignment to try and create different shapes, or they can be presented with a story. One popular story related to the Tangram puzzle is a story about an old man Tan, who was carrying a tile. Unfortunately, he dropped the tile and it broke into seven pieces. Tan tried to put the pieces together, but instead the pieces were falling into amazing shapes of boats, plants, animals, birds, etc. At this point students are shown some of these shapes and are invited to recreate them using a replica of the broken pieces of Tan's tile.

The features of the tile (beautiful, heavy, glass or marble), the circumstances that made Tan carry it (as a gift for his lady, as a sacrifice to his gods, as a stolen item from an ancient museum), and then drop it (minor earthquake, slipped on a banana peel, a beautiful girl passed by) remain unclear. They can be filled in by the story teller or the story listeners to make the story more interesting and engaging. Filling in these details can even be extended as an imaginative writing assignment. A more elaborated version is found in the children's book *Granfather's Tang's Story* by Ann Tompert and Robert Parker (Tompert & Parker, 1997). Now compare and contrast the story of Tan with the tale of Quint of Fredan.

> *Until a month ago Quint had led a perfectly normal existence in the town of Fredan on the most southern peninsula of Groulax. He spent the days working in his father's urn store and the evenings sitting around a fire on the beach with his friends. Life was perfectly normal – and boring. Quint wanted an adventure, he constantly dreamed about fighting beasts, doing battle with the gods, conquering distant lands, and falling in love with a beautiful princess. Now those dreams were the thing of reality, and although he would like nothing more than to be back in the safety of his father's store he was not about to abandon the princess to the hideous beast that stood before him. This was only the most recent of the monsters he had had to do battle with. He had already outwitted the cunning Snorlax of Equinon, slaved the dreaded Gradou, and outrun the lumbering Vernid in the forest of Andour. This time, however, his luck had run out. The Demon Joust had disarmed him with little effort and had cut off his only means of escape with a single wave of his wand. Death was imminent. "You love the princess, this is clear", said the demon, "you would die for her. But would*

you give your eternal soul to spare her life?" Quint stood fast, he knew the legend of Joust and the seemingly simple but in fact rather difficult tasks Joust enjoyed giving his rivals. "What do you propose?" asked Quint. "We will give you a Tangram, or set of 7 geometric shapes, and you will have exactly 7 minutes to build 7 animals of my choice from these shapes. If you succeed, both you and the princess go free. If you lose, however, I keep your eternal soul."

We consider the story of a broken tile as one that intertwines with mathematical content, while the story of Quint serves as a frame or background. That is to say, While Tan's story is connected to the subsequent activity, Quint could have been presented with any other challenge. In fact, teachers can use the Quint story, or any variation of it, and present any task as Quint's challenge.

Many different plots can create a fitting frame or a nice background story. As long as the heroes face challenges and overcome obstacles, the problems that they solve along the way can be related to the standard mathematics curriculum.

A story is not the only possible frame for disguising a curriculum activity. Resourceful teachers have integrated mathematical problems in games like Jeopardy and activities like a scavenger hunt. In fact, most stories that exist in mathematical 'folklore' and are either written in books or are passed from one generation to another by teachers and fans of mathematics are related to 'fun' or extracurricular mathematics and not to the 'nuts and bolts' of daily life in a mathematics classroom. For example, the story about multiplying rabbits (to introduce the Fibonacci sequence) or about crossing the bridges of Konigsberg (to introduce Euler's circuit in graphs) intertwine with the content and may lead to fruitful and exciting mathematical activity, but this activity is not at the heart of the current school curriculum. There are no 'classical' or well known stories that help with the tortures of long division or factoring, with adding fractions or performing operations with integers, respecting the order of operations. That is where a frame or a background story, though not our first choice for engagement, could be very helpful.

There are three main types of stories that frame. One is that of heroes who have to overcome obstacles to reach their goal. The story of Quint and the story of the Sphinx and her riddle presented above are such examples. Likely, the most popular framing story is that of Sheherazade in the book of a *One Thousand and One Arabian Nights*. The story is that every day king Shahryar married a new virgin, and the next day sent her to be beheaded. This was an act of revenge for his first wife's betrayal. Sheherazade was one of the virgins that Shahryar married, but foreseeing her destiny, she started to tell the king a story. But it was not just any story, it was a story of adventure and intrigue, of suspense and surprise, of thieves and of kings. In addition, Sheherazade had perfect timing: Just as she got to the moment of greatest suspense ... the night ended. So Shahryar kept Sheherazade alive for the next day, eager to know how the story ended. The next night, as one story ended, another exciting story started, that again thrilled and intrigued the king. And so he kept Sheherazade alive for yet another day. And this pattern continued for a thousand and one nights, by which time Sheherazade and Shahryar

CHAPTER 4

had three sons. (It appears that storytelling and story listening was not their only entertainment.)

Though the book of one thousand and one nights is a very specific collection of Persian and Middle Eastern folklore, any story – as long as it caught Shahryar's interest – could fit into this frame. The fact is that the most famous stories of Arabian and Persian origin – such as *The Magic Lamp of Aladdin* or *Ali Baba and the 40 Thieves* – are not in the original Arabic version of the book; they were added to the collection by European translators in early nineteenth century.

Regarding Sheherazade, we would be remiss if we do not mention that there is also an explicit mathematical connection. Inspired by 1001 in *One Thousand and One Nights*, some refer to palindromic numbers as Sheherazade numbers. Palindromic numbers are symmetrical numbers, those that read the same from left to right as right to left, such as 121, 13531, or 5665. Elementary school students could be invited to determine how many 2- or 3-digit Sheherazade numbers there are. In upper grades this count could be extended to more digits. Could it be that Shahryar started to count 4-digit Sheherazade numbers, but fell asleep? Or maybe he was interested in palindromic primes or palindromic perfect squares? Time can be found for some recreational mathematics inspired by Sheherazade.

A second kind of a framing story is that of a secret code. A coded message can be left anywhere by anyone and found anywhere by anyone. And decoding the message can save lives, or point to a treasure, win a princess' heart, or ensure fame and glory. However, decoding the message can involve any curriculum-based task, such as solving equations or determining volumes of pyramids. A story can tell about students discovering an ancient Egyptian papyrus in their back yard, and striving to interpret the symbols, rather than simply being presented with the Egyptian numeration system. A story can tell about a hidden message that is decoded by matching numbers with digits or words, where the numbers are results of calculations to be practiced at any given level.

A third kind of a story that serves as a frame is that of a treaty or a contract. The idea is presented by Haven (2000), as he describes helping a third grade teacher to create a story for teaching multiplication. In this story Ms. Multiplicand behaved in such a way that no one was willing to work with her. However, she herself could not do all the multiplying work at hand, and this frustrated the King of Numbers. So the king ordered everyone involved in multiplication work to cooperate and create a treaty that precisely described the role of each player. This treaty then became the algorithm for multiplication that the teacher planned to introduce that day.

In such a way a treaty can describe many different rules and processes. Consider for example the order of operations. Once upon a time the operations got into a war over order, where each one wanted to be carried out before the others. The King of Numbers, who was fond of tennis, suggested that this game could help in setting the order once and for all. The first game was to be played in pairs – Multiplication and Division against Addition and Subtraction. It was a close game, but Multiplication and Division were the victors. As such, the King decided they would be performed first. But which one? Being the inverses of each other, they didn't want to give up. So they played another game of tennis, this time Multiplication played against Division. The game went on for several days without a winner being declared. Both players exhibited equally strong powers. Surprisingly or not, the same happened in the game between Addition and Subtraction. So the King imposed the following contract: Multiplication and Division shall be performed before Addition and Subtraction, but in the order in which they appear in any calculation. Addition and Subtraction will follow, again respecting the order in which they are listed. In this way, in some tasks multiplication will be ahead of division, while in other tasks it will follow division. Similarly, respectful of the order, in some tasks addition will be performed before subtraction, while in other tasks it will be performed after. This appears fair, all the operations agreed and signed the contract.

Recently at MacDonald's, a customer had to demonstrate the skill on a 'skill testing question' in order to be eligible for a prize – a small Coke or a small fries. The skill testing question asked the customer to evaluate $100 - 40 \div 5$. One customer offered the answer of 92. "Indeed," mentioned the cashier, "this is one of the correct answers." The customer appeared surprised. "What do you mean by 'one of the correct answers'?" The cashier offered a friendly smile. "There are two possible answers", she claimed, "one is 92, the other is 12, which most customers get by the way". Obviously, neither the cashier, nor "most customers" were actively aware of the treaty signed among the Operations and the King of Numbers.

'BEDMAS' (acronym for Brackets, Exponents, Division, Multiplication, Addition, Subtraction) is a popular reference in North America that supposingly helps students memorize the order of operations. However, this 'help' also presents a danger. It implies, for example, that addition precedes subtraction and division precedes multiplication.

Returning to the 'treaty' as a possible framing story, a word of warning is in order. Treaties may serve well to represent conventions, where there is no logical derivation for the rules we live by. Order of operations or the choice of positive direction for the axes of coordinates are examples of such conventions. Standard computational algorithms are not. These algorithms are not based on arbitrary choices, but derived through logic and reason. What appears arbitrary, however, are the curriculum choices made as to which algorithm is taught in school, because for each algorithm taught there are several alternatives developed in different cultures.

We will be saddened if formulas or theorems, that can be derived logically, are presented as a 'treaty'. For example, formulas for calculating areas of geometric shapes or volumes of solids, formulas for 'short multiplication' or laws of operations with exponents can be developed building on prior knowledge of students. In these cases 'treaties' may do more harm than good.

Without dismissing the value of stories that serve as a frame for mathematical engagement, we seek stories that are more closely related to mathematics to be explored and understood. Thus, in the following chapters we explore stories that intertwine with mathematical activity, that introduce ideas or explain concepts, and that ask questions.

CHAPTER 5

STORIES THAT ACCOMPANY
AND
STORIES THAT INTERTWINE

ARCHIMEDES: MAKING THE DISTINCTION

Remember Archimedes? There are several famous stories about him. One tells about Archimedes having a bath and observing the rising level of the water. This led to his discovery of 'Archimedes' Law of Buoyancy[*]'. According to the well-known legend, Archimedes was so excited with this discovery, that he jumped out of the bath tub and ran naked through the streets of Syracuse shouting 'Eureka', meaning in Greek, "I found it". What he had found was a way of measuring the volume of a sacred wreath, allegedly made of pure gold, to determine whether the goldsmith had replaced some of the gold with other, less valuable, metal.

Another story is about Archimedes' death. A popular version of the legend, described in further detail in Chapter 2, tells that Archimedes was killed by a Roman soldier while drawing a geometrical diagram in the sand. As the soldier approached, his shadow covered part of the diagram, and Archimedes told the soldier "Noli turbare circulos meos" ("Do not disturb my circles"). The soldier could not bear the insult and killed the man who dared to show him such disrespect. Another variation of the story tells us that the soldier suggested to Archimedes to move out of his way, but Archimedes refused to leave before finishing the problem he was investigating.

Both stories are pure fiction, but historical truth is not of our concern here. Fact or fiction aside, both stories build on the ingenious human qualities of our hero. One is excitement with discovery to the level of euphoria, a state in which an individual is so overwhelmed with pleasure that he is no longer thinking logically about his actions. Another is a profound engagement in a mathematical activity, to the exclusion of the reality that surrounds him. These human qualities engage the imaginations of learners, young and old, and we shall return to them several times in this book. Here we would like to point out an important difference between the two stories. The second story is about a man. The first story is not only about a man but also about science and mathematics. While the second story ends, the first one may evolve into the introduction of concepts such as volume and buoyancy or a continuation of the investigation of these concepts. With these two examples in

---

[*]A body submerged in a fluid experiences a buoyant force equal to the weight of the displaced fluid.

mind we distinguish between stories that *accompany* the content and stories that *intertwine* with the content. There exists an abundance of materials, mostly with reference to the history of mathematics and to the lives of mathematicians, from which to derive stories that accompany (e.g., NCTM, 1989). Stories that intertwine, in which mathematical content emerges through the story, at times leaving the story behind and at times staying with the story, are harder to find. But it is in the teacher's hands to invent those stories and use them for the benefit of learning. Having made the distinction, in what follows we tell stories of different kinds.

ARCHIMEDES REVISITED: EXEMPLIFYING THE DISTINCTION

Recall the story of Archimedes' naked run through the streets of Syracuse. As mentioned in Chapter 2, casting different characters as 'opposites' to each other enhances the impact of the story on the listeners and learners. This particular story can be told in a variety of different ways casting different characters against each other in order to draw students' attention and provoke their emotions one way or another (Egan, 1997). Consider, for example, a version where Archimedes is seen as a town eccentric, well known for his inattentiveness to personal hygiene. The town's people plot a bath for this unkempt member of their society. On the fateful day they abduct Archimedes from his home, ceremoniously carry him through the streets to the local bathhouse, strip him naked, and begin the bath. No sooner is he submerged in the tub than he jumps out again, screams 'Eureka' at the poor bathhouse attendant and proceeds to run back to his home, naked. Such a telling casts the rational town's people against the eccentric mathematician and, thus serves to accentuate the eccentric nature of mathematicians. Deepening the plot can further polarize these feelings.

For example, we can mention the young family who lives in the room above that of Archimedes. It was the pleas of the mother to the town council that initiated the whole 'bathe the mathematician' campaign. You see, the stench that rose through the floorboard was making her life unbearable. Her daughter had stopped eating because of it and had subsequently fallen ill. Casting this poor innocent young family against the irrationality of Archimedes would very effectively move a listener's emotions to side with the town's people.

However, we could also mention that Archimedes was working on a problem for the king that was most pressing. Recall the gold wreath – the goldsmith who had made it was a travelling goldsmith and he was leaving town in a matter of days. The king had charged Archimedes with the task of determining whether all the gold had indeed been used, or had been substituted with a less valuable metal. This task came with a very dire consequence should he fail. If the goldsmith left before Archimedes solved the problem then he would be forced to leave Syracuse forever. At the point in the story of the bath Archimedes had been working on the problem nonstop for five days, only stopping to eat a little bit. He had not slept, and he had certainly not bathed. This time the casting of the poor Archimedes against the tyranny of the king will surely sway a listener's allegiance to that of Archimedes.

Each of these versions is engaging in its own way, but they are equally lacking in one regard. They do not draw the students' attention or emotion in a direction that is even remotely related to mathematics. This is often the hallmark of stories that introduce. They are sort of a one-hit wonder that captures the imagination of the students. Well crafted with the use of thoughtfully constructed binary opposites such a story can serve to provide an impetus to propel students into a topic. However, if we want to ensure this we need to move the story from one that introduces to one that asks a question or one that intertwines. A possible question here could be, "The water in the bath was rising. How much did it rise? And what happened to the water when our hero jumped out of the bath?" These questions could lead to the experiment of placing different objects in containers with water, measuring the displacement and developing a hypothesis.

While good stories are an excellent tool to enrich the classroom, we are most interested in stories that support learning. Recall the story of Archimedes, Bartholomew, and measuring circles. The casting of the relatively onerous and clumsy way of measuring circles as exemplified by Bartholomew versus the elegance of Archimedes' solution is a nice introduction to a variety of lessons including the circumference of a circle, π, Archimedes, ancient woodworking crafts, and ... Jamaica. But it is such a well-crafted story that it would be a shame to leave it as a story that simply introduces. We will show how it can be used to integrate a mathematical activity and how it can be extended to reach deeper into mathematical content.

So first, how can this story intertwine with a mathematical activity? We can start by measuring circles using Bartholomew's method. Have each student consider something circular. This can be a coin, a cup, a plate, a garbage can – anything that can be brought to or found in class, and a variety of sizes of these circles is appreciated. Have students measure the diameter and the perimeter (circumference) of these circles and record their finding in a table. This table may look as follows:

	Circumference (C)	Diameter (D)	C:D
coin	68mm	23mm	2.96
garbage can	185 cm	57 cm	3.25
glass	10 paperclips	3 paperclips	3.3
plate	682mm	213mm	3.2
carpet design	14 meters	5 meters	2.8
CD	28 fingers	9 fingers	3.11
globe model	?	?	3.07

Having completed the table, we suggest asking students if they notice anything interesting, or, whether given the diameter they can guess or approximate the perimeter, or, whether it seems reasonable, based on the data compiled, to have a diameter of 7 and the circumference of 46. From this activity, we would like students to notice that the numbers recorded for circumference are approximately 3 times larger than the numbers for diameter. It may be helpful to fill in the columns

CHAPTER 5

for circumference and diameter first and only after a hypothesis of relationship between the two is formulated to fill in the additional column – the ratio of perimeter to diameter. Is it possible to create a circle in which the perimeter to diameter ratio is about 7?

That could be a way of introducing one of the magical constants in mathematics – the number π and its commonly used approximations. For all the practical purposes of school, the value of this number can be taken as 22/7 or 3.14. But where did it come from? Where do all the constants and formulas come from? For most learners, they come from the teachers or from the back of the textbook. Students learn to apply them correctly, but do they wonder how and when these formulas were introduced? Calculating the circumference knowing the number and the relationship (formula) is one task, but coming up with the value for this wonderful number is another. So, how can the value of π be determined? We have already seen that tying ropes around circular objects does not give a very precise estimate. Is there another way?

Of course, it is possible to tell stories, as we often do, about the great achievements of others. It is more challenging – but we believe also more rewarding – to have students relive the experience of others. Having students follow the method of Archimedes and estimate π by inscribing and circumscribing polygons – this method is described in a story in Chapter 2 – and maybe competing for the most accurate estimate is a possible activity. However, we acknowledge a practical difficulty in constructing regular polygons and therefore we continue our story to avoid this problem. This time we reverse the polarity of the binary opposites and attempt to forge an allegiance with Bartholomew.

Before Bartholomew retired, however, he managed to teach Archimedes a thing or three himself. You see, as brilliant as Archimedes was, he was obsessed with symmetry. Everything about Archimedes' life was symmetrical. He even learned to write with both hands so that he could satisfy his obsession. Because of this, when Archimedes started his own circle measuring business he would spend an inordinate amount of time making sure the polygons he inscribed and circumscribed in his circle were perfectly symmetrical. He was making what we call regular polygons. Now, Bartholomew, although a little slow to keep up with new technology, was no dummy. He eventually picked up this new trick and before long he was back in business. Only he seemed to be measuring circles much faster than Archimedes. Archimedes just assumed that Bartholomew was doing an inferior job of it and that was why he was so quick. But what Archimedes hadn't figured out and Bartholomew had, was that the polygons did not have to be regular in order to get a pretty good measurement of the circumference of a circle. Was he right?

With that we segue into a very nice activity. We engage students in estimating the circumference of the circle by constructing – inscribing and circumscribing – regular quadrilaterals (squares) and irregular ones, and then measuring and averaging their perimeters. Then we turn to pentagons, hexagons, etc. The students should not use precise construction tools to make regular polygons, but ultimately, some polygons look 'more regular' than the others. After combining students' results and ideas, the story can continue.

> *As it turned out Bartholomew was right. Sure sometimes he had to draw more straight lines to get a good measurement, but that didn't bother him in the least. What is important is that his latest technological advancement earned him enough money to retire to Jamaica. Meanwhile, back in Syracuse Archimedes was forging ahead with his own work. With the latest advancements at his fingertips he was now able to address the problem of his real passion for circles – the calculation of the special relationship between the circumference of a circle and its diameter.*

At this point we will leave the story safe in the knowledge that Archimedes eventually found this special relationship. Incidentally, although we may have embellished a little on the details of the story, the truth is that Archimedes' method of calculating π – the constant ratio of the circumference of a circle to its diameter – stood as the most accurate one used up until the 17th century, when the creation of calculus produced a better estimate. By inscribing and circumscribing polygons in a circle – as the story suggests in Chapter 2 – Archimedes estimated π correctly to 2 decimal places. His wonderfully accurate – considering the tools – estimate, made at about 300 B.C.E. was:

$$3\frac{1}{7} > \frac{14688}{4673\frac{1}{2}} > \pi > \frac{6336}{2017\frac{1}{4}} > 3\frac{10}{71}$$

Using only the first six digits beyond the decimal point, we get
$$3.142857 > 3.142827 > \pi > 3.140910 > 3.140845$$
which gives the value of π accurate to the 2 decimal places.

In fact, determining the exact value of π attracted the best minds of mathematics. Today we know that π is an irrational number, that is, there is an infinite amount of digits in its decimal expansion and there is no repeating pattern in these digits. Several millions of these digits have been computed using advanced computer technology and sophisticated algorithms. Such detailed computations have little practical value in that we do not need to know the millionth digit of π for the building of arches and the design of aircrafts and spaceships. However, a very powerful force drives people to design even-more powerful ways of calculating the digits – the sense of wonder. But this is a different story.

In this final part of our story about Archimedes and Bartholomew, several binary opposites can be capitalized upon: sloppy versus precise constructions, symmetrical versus asymmetrical polygons, tedious versus efficient calculations. Following these characters we demonstrated how a story can be extended from one that introduces to one that intertwines and reaches deep into the subject matter.

CHAPTER 6

STORIES THAT INTRODUCE

There are stories that serve well to introduce concepts or ideas and there are stories that we use as an introduction or trigger for a mathematical activity. Many stories can serve a dual purpose of introducing both concepts and activities. Several such stories are told in this chapter.

ANNO'S MYSTERIOUS MULTIPLYING JAR: A STORY OF FACTORIAL

As an example of a story that introduces a concept consider *Anno's Mysterious Multiplying Jar* (Anno & Anno, 1983). This wonderful children's book with big pictures and only a few lines of text tells about a jar within which there was a rippling sea. On the sea there was one island; on the island there were 2 countries; within each country there were 3 mountains; on each mountain there were 4 walled kingdoms; within each walled kingdom there were 5 villages; in each village there were 6 houses; in each house there were 7 rooms; in each room there were 8 cupboards; within each cupboard there were 9 boxes; within each box there were 10 jars. So how many jars were there in all the boxes altogether? This question mark is an appropriate place to pause in the reading of the book. Although the book continues by introducing the idea of factorial and its mathematical symbol (!) we suggest departing from the book at this point and seeking students' help in figuring out the answer. The pattern and the concept can be developed by systematically showing the number of each entity:

$2 \times 1 = 2! = 2$ the number of countries
$3 \times 2 \times 1 = 3! = 6$ the number of mountains
$4 \times 3 \times 2 \times 1 = 4! = 24$ the number of walled kingdoms

A few more lines could be used to introduce an amazing and surprisingly large number 3,628,800 : $10 \times 9 \times 8 \times 7 \times 6 \times 5 \times 4 \times 3 \times 2 \times 1 = 10! = 3,628,800$

This symbolic representation is more meaningful when accompanied by a visual image representing this magnitude. Therefore, these calculations would have greater power to engage learners' imagination if accompanied with a visual representation of 2, 6, 24, 120, etc. dots. Of course, for teachers who are eager to save time, the concept of factorial can be introduced with the one-line definition:
n! is a product of natural numbers from 1 to n, or, $n! = 1 \times 2 \times 3 \times 4 \times \ldots \times n$. However, as is definitely clear to the reader by now, we believe in the power of spending time on storytelling, choosing stories that serve the learning of mathematics.

CHAPTER 6

Once the idea of factorial is established, and students have calculated 5!, 8!, 10! And maybe even 12!, a related story can be told. And this is a true story.

Once upon a time, shortly after computers were first developed, they were not of a size to fit on your lap or be held in your palm. They occupied several rooms. Some time in the middle of the 20th century, a group of mathematically inclined students were introduced to the magic of computer programming. This was done without a computer of course. Instead, the program was written on paper and checked by following the commands, imagining how a computer would execute it. One day these students were permitted to visit a computer facility at the local University and be allowed to have the big computer execute the programs they had written. Because computers were pretty scarce and computer time rather expensive, this was considered to be a real treat. Of course the time at the facility was limited and programs had been carefully assigned by the teacher. However, as it often happens, one of the students finished the assignment before the others, and rather than waiting for his classmates in boredom, wrote a program that was supposed to calculate 100! It was rather simple and looked something like that:

```
counter = 1
factorial = 1
  while counter < 101
    factorial = factorial * counter
    counter = counter + 1
end
```

The big computer got stuck. The number was too large for it to handle. It took several hours for the technician to put the computer back into working condition. The student was expelled from the computer course. And it took three years until the teacher was able yet again to organize a trip to the computer facility at the University for her students. Believe it or not, this is a true story.

The magnitude of numbers is often not only beyond our imagination, but also beyond computational abilities of machines. Today's computers will not get stuck calculating 100!, but will likely report an error when 1,000,000! is sought. Students often like to test the computational limits of their calculators. Fortunately, they do not get stuck when pushed beyond their limits. They simply give us an error message.

Our next story also deals with big numbers, numbers that start small but grow quickly.

GRAINS ON A CHESSBOARD: A STORY OF EXPONENTIAL GROWTH

Big numbers are often a source of fascination. Some young children wonder what the biggest number is and how long would it take to count up to it. Others are amazed by how quickly large numbers may emerge from simple patterns. One such pattern, exponential growth, is a source of wonder even for those who accepted the idea of an infinity of natural numbers long ago. A classical story that introduces the idea of exponential growth has many shapes. The core of the story has to do with a sad or bored king and the ingenious creator of the game of chess. So...

> *Once upon a time there was a king. Some say that the king was simply bored and he sought entertainment and intellectual challenge. Others say that the king was depressed because even though he had recently won a big war against invaders from the neighbouring kingdom, his dear son lost his life in the battle. Be it one way or the other, the king's advisors sought a way to cheer the king up. Maybe this was their loyal duty and part of the job description, or maybe they were worried because the depressed king was ignoring the matters of the kingdom. Be it one way or the other, men came from far and wide bringing with them different attractions in an attempt to entertain the king. There was two headed snake, a dwarf that could balance 18 beer bottles on his toe and Hyper-Nintendo with seven controllers... But nothing engaged the king. Until one man brought the game of chess.*

If you buy into the version of the story that talks about the lost son, you may add, for those familiar with chess, that the game was created in order to convince the king that at times it is necessary to sacrifice an officer in order to win a battle. Anyway, back to the story.

> *The king loved the game. No, not just loved – admired, became addicted to it – and requested that all his staff and family learn to play chess, and hosted prestigious chess tournaments. Some say that Bobby Fischer was one of the descendants of this king.*

> *So the king called the inventor of the game and offered him the choice of any gift or prestigious post on the king's staff. But the man didn't wish for any of this. All he asked for was some wheat. In particular, he asked for one grain of wheat for the first square on chess board, two grains of wheat for the second square on the chess board, 4 grains of wheat for the third square, 8 for the fourth, 16 for the fifth, 32 for the next one, and so on, for each square of the board. The king was rather surprised with what he perceived as rather modest request; he immediately called his advisors and asked them to calculate the amount of grains to be given to the chess inventor.*

Pause here. Do not hurry. Some teachers tend to give out the answer too quickly. We suggest allowing the students to carry out the calculation. After all, unlike the king's advisors, they do have calculators. Inevitably, the students will give up, overwhelmed by the enormity of the numbers. Only then the story may continue to its conclusion.

> *The day after the king assigned his advisors to calculate the amount of grain needed there was no response, no answer was forthcoming. Five days later, there still was no answer. Ten days later they brought the king rather strange news: there was not enough grain in all the kingdom to satisfy the man's request. What would the king do? Apologize for not being able to*

CHAPTER 6

> *fulfill the request? Execute the man for his arrogant request? Appoint the chess inventor as his personal adviser on matters of mathematics and games?*

A story teller will decide how the story ends. One version of this story is featured in the book *The King's Chessboard* by David Birch (Birch, 1993). Several variations and possible extensions of this story are presented in Chapter 12. In another popular contemporary variation on the story in the book *One Grain of Rice* by Demi, the chess inventor is a young female and in lieu of the grain, rice in this case, the king will feed the people of her village for a hundred years. Some tellers may prefer this twist. As for the students, they may keep wondering for years how such a simple-looking calculation results in such large numbers. We have witnessed students who were presented with the answer before being given the opportunity to try and figure it out, but they kept trying to calculate the number, in a way intuitively rejecting acceptance of such a magnitude.

A FLY ON A CEILING: A STORY OF CARTESIAN COORDINATES.

Cartesian coordinates are often thought of in school as X-Y axes. The power of a coordinate system is in creating one-to-one correspondence between an ordered pair of (real) numbers and a point on a plane. The introduction of the coordinate system by Rene Descartes in the 17th century was a revolutionary idea that bridged Algebra and Geometry, creating what is known today as Analytic Geometry. Before embedding this idea in mathematics, Algebra and Geometry were thought of as unrelated fields of study. The coordinate system created the opportunity to represent geometric curves as algebraic equations, and this presented a new lens for the study of their properties.

Many revolutionary inventions can be introduced with a story. We have already mentioned Archimedes and his bathtub. It is also said that Newton was resting under an apple tree when an apple fell on his head, an event that triggered the development of the theory of gravity. But what about Descartes?

The legend tells us that Descartes was taking a rest from his philosophical thoughts, lying in bed and staring at the ceiling. He noticed that a fly was moving on the ceiling, crawling in different directions. He wondered how one can best describe the location of the fly. He closed his eyes, and opened them again, and had an inspiration: he could describe the location of the fly by indicating its distance from two adjacent walls. This led to the invention of the system of coordinates, referred today as Cartesian coordinates in his honour.

This story can be preceded or followed up with an activity: There is a sandbox in the middle of the class and a 'treasure' (can be a coin) buried in it. What is the best way to describe the location of the treasure? Students can practice giving precise directions to each other, before turning to plotting points on a graph paper.

The fly on the ceiling sparks the introduction of coordinate systems. The story also tells us that taking a rest from an intellectual engagement – either lying in bed or under an apple tree – can lead to exciting inventions.

STORIES THAT INTRODUCE

PIRATES AND BURIED TREASURE: A STORY OF A STANDARD UNIT

It often happens in a mathematics classroom that a concept is introduced before the need for this concept is established. This is problematic. However, a story may help in creating the need for a concept. Consider for example a story of buried treasure.

> *A pirate on his dying bed whispered to his sons: "There is a great treasure that I buried in the Forest of Darkville. Starting at the back door of the Old Church, take 400 paces North and then 300 paces East. You will reach a big oak tree – the treasure is right there."*
>
> *So the sons rushed to Darkville. The older son, starting at the back door of the Old Church took 400 paces North and then 300 paces East. But he found himself in the middle of a meadow, there were no oak trees around. Was his father hallucinating?*
>
> *The younger son, starting at the back door of the Old Church took 400 paces North and then 300 paces East. There was an oak tree close by. It was not a very big tree, but, who knows, maybe it appeared big to the father. The young son started digging. Deeper and deeper. But he found no treasure. He recounted the steps, this time finishing on the other side of the tree, and dug again. But the treasure was not to be found. Was his father forgetting something? Or maybe he had not heard well as his father's voice was weak. Maybe his father had meant the forest of Oakville rather than the forest of Darkville? Or maybe he said 600 paces and not 300 paces?*

Pause. Let us ask the students to help us find the treasure. We believe that among a variety of suggestions, at least one would focus on the size of one's paces. Indeed, the father was a short man. But he was strong and powerful, so that the sons did not think of him as small. Nonetheless, his steps were short. But how short?

We suggest letting the students continue the story. Maybe the sons just tried shorter paces and found the treasure. And maybe they never did. Maybe they asked their uncle, who was about the same height as their father to help and shared the treasure with him. Or maybe a short nurse overheard the pirate's last words and made her way to the treasure long before the sons did.

Aside from imaginative story telling, the question we would like students to consider is what the pirate could have done to assure his sons get the treasure. We believe that the idea of a common unit of measure – be it a family cane or a length of a rope around the family well – will surface in discussion with students. This idea can further be developed in the introduction and appreciation of a 'standard' unit – standard within one's family, standard within one's classroom, or standard universally.

While the pirate story can introduce the idea and the concept of a standard unit, it can also be used to introduce the concept of proportion and a related activity. This can develop as follows: Suppose that the father's paces were 45 cm long, and the son's paces are 60 cm long. How many paces should the son make to equal 300

CHAPTER 6

paces of his father? Of course, one can dig under all the oak trees in the area, but some mathematical engagement may save work and hasten the path to the treasure.

As we mentioned earlier, our classification of stories into different categories is not clear cut. Some stories fall into more than one category as they can be used for more than one purpose. The pirate story in this section can be used to introduce an idea (standard unit) and can be used to introduce an activity (determining length using proportion). In the next section we discuss several stories that serve as an introduction for a mathematical activity.

COUNTING AN ARMY: A STORY OF POSITIONAL DECIMAL SYSTEM

We often take our numeration system and the standard measurement systems for granted, either forgetting or being totally unaware of the fact that the invention and the cultural acceptance and dissemination of the positional decimal (Hindu-Arabic) number system was a serious breakthrough in the development of arithmetic. To recreate and, as a result, accentuate this breakthrough Egan (1986) uses the example of a king who wanted to count his army. We present an abbreviated version of the story here.

> *The king had a whole cadre of clueless counsellors and one ingenious counsellor. The clueless counsellors tried to count soldiers one by one, but they kept losing count. They tried using the shepherd's method of placing one stone in a pile for every soldier that marched past, but there were not enough stones in the field where they were camped. So, after having watched the repeated bunglings of his clueless counsellors, the king turned to his most ingenious counsellor. The ingenious counsellor implemented the following strategy:*
>
> *In front of each clueless counsellor was placed a bowl and ten pebbles. The army then began to march past the end of the table. As each soldier went by, the first counsellor put one pebble into his bowl. Once he had put all ten pebbles into the bowl, he scooped them up and then continued to put one pebble down for each soldier marching by the table. He had a very busy afternoon, putting down his pebbles one by one and then scooping them up when all were in the bowl. Each time he scooped up the ten pebbles, the clueless counsellor to his left put one pebble into her bowl. When her ten pebbles were in her bowl, she too scooped them out again, and continued to put one back into the bowl each time the clueless counsellor to her right picked his up.*
>
> *The clueless counsellor to her left had to watch her through the afternoon, and he put one pebble into his bowl each time she picked hers up. And so on for the remaining counsellors.*
>
> *At the end of the afternoon, the counsellor on the far left had only one pebble in his bowl, the next counsellor had two, the next had seven, the next had six and the counsellor at the other end of the table, where the soldiers*

had marched by, had three pebbles in his bowl. So we know that the army had 12,763 men. The king was delighted that his ingenious counsellor had counted the whole army with just fifty pebbles.

Students, as listeners, can effectively associate with the ingenuity of the strategy presented by the clever counsellor, especially when the story is shaped to build on the abstract binary opposites of clueless vs. ingenious counsellors, or ineffective vs. efficient methods of counting. Furthermore, this story can provide access to, or reinforcement of, the idea of place value.

However, rather than letting children become observers of ingenuity, teachers can invite them to become ingenious creators themselves. Rather than presenting them with the ideas of the clever counsellor, let us ask students to suggest a strategy for counting large quantities. The setting of the story can vary considerably, and we consider below one possible variation.

Recall the story of Amzula and his sheep from Chapter 1 in this book. In the beginning, Amzula assured himself that all the sheep returned home by putting a pebble in his bag for each sheep that went out and taking this pebble out of the bag when sheep returned later that evening. This strategy was adopted by his descendants. But the sheep were fruitful and multiplied, and the people of Zalla eventually learned how to count. One day the chief-shepherd wanted to know how many sheep there were. He tried to count the sheep as they walked out of their pen, but kept getting confused. So he got out his trusted pebbles, and began to place them in his bag as they left the pen.

We suggest presenting students with a 'large' amount of objects (marbles, beans, popsicle sticks). This 'large' amount can vary from about 40 to over a thousand, depending on the students' level. The students' task becomes then not just to count the objects, but to arrange them in such a way that a partner can verify the count easily. We expect that ideas of grouping – but not necessarily grouping in tens – will emerge. For example, in order to guide a partner towards easy verification of 47 beans, one can arrange them in 9 groups of 5 and 2 more. By considering different ways of arranging objects in groups and the varying degree to which these arrangements contribute to the ease of counting, students will eventually tend towards groupings of ten. At some point even the numbers of groupings of ten may become too large to attend to. Hopefully, at this stage a student will suggest to arrange 10 groups of 10 in a group of 100.

Congratulations. The decimal numeration system has just been reinvented. Reinvented as a result of the need not only to count large amounts, but also to be able to verify the count. And the ingenious suggestion is credited to a group of students, rather than a clever, but nameless, counsellor.

PLANET PENTA: A STORY OF BASE 5

Computations in different bases are usually not part of the core school curriculum. However, the topic can be used in special enhanced curriculum classrooms. This is also a popular theme in classes for prospective teachers.

CHAPTER 6

How can the idea of different bases be introduced? By inviting students to join a trip to a different planet. On this planet – we call it Penta for now, but any other name can be considered – similar to Earth, intelligent life forms have developed. Surprisingly or not, they are very much like humans: they eat Pizza, they drive cars and they send their children to schools. They even look very similar to us humans, the main difference is that their legs have no toes and they have only one hand. But, like us, they have 5 fingers on their one hand. Resembling humans, they invented a place value computation, however, they developed it using their 5 fingers. So, in our symbols, they would say 1, 2, 3, 4 ... but rather that 5 they say 10.

Activities that evolve after this introduction involve counting in base 5, converting numbers from base 5 to base 10 and performing numerical operations. Every task can be set with reference to Penta. For example, visiting Penta, one may look for 'classified' ads and find a single female, 42 years old. This age is in base 5 of course. How old is she really? (Is she of legal age?) Or, being invited to give a guest lecture, a professor is told to expect an audience of about 240 people. Should she be ready to face a large auditorium or a small classroom? How many handouts should she prepare? Any conversion problem can be set in a humorous situation.

Having explored Penta, the tourists can be invited to visit different planets and practice their skills in bases other-than-five.

SUMMARY

In Chapters 5 and 6 we drew a distinction between stories that simply introduce or accompany mathematics and stories that intertwine, that serve as a springboard to engage learners in mathematical exploration. 'Mathematics' here is interpreted broadly – it can be a specific mathematical algorithm (Gauss pairing method), concept (π, exponential growth, decimal notation, factorial) or an activity (Tangram), but it can also be a way of thinking (relying on a previously solved problem), or a human need for creating an idea (standard unit).

CHAPTER 7

STORIES THAT EXPLAIN

Mathematics is often perceived by learners as a collection of facts and skills; facts and skills that are sometimes seen as counterintuitive. When this happens a common reaction is to seek refuge in the meaningless memorization of rules. Experienced teachers can easily point to such places, places in which encounters with mathematics are most puzzling and rules are most prevalent. Instead of reciting rules, however, we suggest explaining these rules with stories. This introduces a new kind of stories – stories that explain. Division by zero, division by a fraction, and the manipulation of negative integers are but a few examples of concepts that students find hard to understand and teachers find even harder to explain. We attempt to explain these with a story. We then identify a repeating theme in our stories, the theme of numerical variation, and attend to additional situations in which varying stories may support learning.

STORIES THAT EXPLAIN A CONCEPT

Division by a fraction and the confused tailor

Algorithmically, division by a fraction is not a problematic issue – *ours is not to reason why, just invert and multiply*. Conceptually, however, division by a fraction is very problematic, leaving learners to memorize the rule and reinforcing the perception that mathematics is but a collection of rules. The mechanics of the rule are best explained as a 'shortcut' for a process that involves mixing representations, compound fractions, and multiplying the numerator and the denominator by the inverse of the denominator For example, consider the following:

$$\frac{3}{4} \div \frac{5}{6} = \frac{\frac{3}{4}}{\frac{5}{6}} = \frac{\frac{3}{4} \times \frac{6}{5}}{\frac{5}{6} \times \frac{6}{5}} = \frac{\frac{3}{4} \times \frac{6}{5}}{1} = \frac{3}{4} \times \frac{6}{5}$$

Even when the technicalities of the 'shortcut' are clear, division by a fraction is still a mystery. On one hand it confronts the common perception, engrained through exposure to division of whole numbers, that "division makes smaller". Numerous research studies have described the strength of this belief and the cognitive conflict that is invoked by exposure to the fact that in some cases, division does not make (the dividend) smaller. On the other hand, many people have difficulty in imagining a situation in which division by fraction is required. Ball (1990) asked elementary school teachers to create a problem that can be

CHAPTER 7

modelled and solved by the following calculation: $2\frac{1}{2} \div \frac{1}{3}$. Only very few participants in her study were successful in creating an appropriate problem. And, in our experience, the task is problematic even to people with significant mathematical background. The majority of people, when asked to write a problem that is modelled with division by a fraction, write stories involving multiplication by a fraction.

To understand why a seemingly simple task leads to erroneous solutions we must sidetrack from our focus on storytelling and consider two different situations involving division. And even before that, we invite the reader to write down a story-problem that can be solved by the following division: 40÷8. Write down something simple, the first thing that comes to mind. We will return to this task shortly.

We now introduce two kinds of division: quotitive and partitive. Imagine 5 baskets with 4 apples in each basket. How many apples are there? The total of 20 is found by multiplication, 4×5. However, if the total is known, two different division problems can be created:

1. There are 20 apples arranged in 5 baskets. How many apples are there in each basket, (assuming that all the baskets have an equal number of apples)?

2. There are 20 apples arranged in baskets such that there are 4 apples in each basket. How many baskets are there?

Problem 1 is an example of partitive division. The amount (20 apples) is arranged in equal parts (baskets). The number of parts is known (5), and the question is asking for the amount in *each* part. This type of a problem is also referred to as the *sharing* model of division.

Problem 2 is an example of quotitive division. Again, the amount (20 apples) is arranged in parts (baskets). However, the number of parts is unknown. What is known is the amount in *each* part. This type of a problem is also referred to as the *measurement* model of division (and in some contexts it can even be referred to as the *scooping* model).

Now we are ready to confront division by a fraction. The problem is, that for most people, the partitive or sharing model of division is a more intuitive one. The situations that come to mind to the majority of people when considering division are partitive. Earlier, we invited the reader to write down a division problem, the first one that comes to mind, for 40÷8. In our experience, most people design a partitive model. That is, the most common problems are those in which 40 people are to sit at 8 tables or 40 candies are to be shared among 8 friends. And this is the source of the problem with division by a fraction – it can only be modeled with a quotitive (measurement) model. So, in order to introduce division by a fraction, we start with a familiar whole number division problem and gradually vary the situation.

Let us say a tailor has 40 yards of fabric and he gets an order for fancy carnival costumes. He decides that 5 yards are needed for each costume. How many costumes can he make? The obvious answer (8) is given by dividing the total amount (40) by the amount needed for one costume (5). This is an example of quotitive division.

Now let us vary the story. The tailor realized that costumes needed to be smaller, and only 4 yards of fabric are necessary to make one costume. How many costumes can he make now? But as he pulled out his scissors to start cutting the fabric, he received a phone call – the order changed. Now, instead of costumes he is to make dresses and each dress requires 2 yards of fabric. And then the order is not for dresses, but for skirts, and each skirt requires one yard of fabric... Starting with the familiar whole number situation we have established that the number of objects (costumes, dresses, skirts, etc) is found by dividing the total amount of fabric by the amount needed for each object. The sequence of division tasks can be recorded as

$40 \div 5 = 8$
$40 \div 4 = 10$
$40 \div 2 = 20$
$40 \div 1 = 40$

We are ready now to move to fractions. If the order is not for skirts, but for aprons, and each apron needs 1/2 of a yard of fabric, how many aprons can be made? This situation is no different from the previous ones, and division by a fraction, $40 \div 1/2$, is smoothly introduced using a story. At this time the amount needed per item can vary. We suggest turning this to students. Let them choose what the tailor makes – ties, scarves, handkerchiefs – and what fraction of a yard each of these objects requires. Corresponding division task will be developed for each suggested order. $40 \div 1/2, 40 \div 1/3, 40 \div 2/3, 40 \div 2/4$, etc.

We believe it is important to leave time for students to figure out the answers to these tasks on their own before introducing the 'invert and multiply' technique. Division by unit fractions presents an obvious link to multiplication. Other fractions should be brought into the story gradually, maybe even not on the same day. In addition to a meaningful introduction to a troublesome concept of division by a fraction, the story achieved another important goal; it helped in confronting the expectation that "division makes smaller" by immersing students in a situation in which the result of division is clearly larger than the dividend.

Division by zero and the king's diamonds

Division by zero is known as yet another problematic issue for learners, young and old. It was also the source of the big Y2K threat. Having survived a few years into the new millennium, however, we have a tendency to forget this.

Division of a number *by zero* is often confused with division *of zero* by another number, creating an erroneous belief that division by zero results in a zero. Mathematically speaking, division by zero is undefined. Often, this idea is interpreted by students inappropriately, claiming that division by zero is an error, infinity, impossible, or 'not allowed'. Each one of these misinterpretations is

CHAPTER 7

problematic on its own. The idea of 'error' comes from the experience of attempting to divide by zero with a calculator in that most calculators will output some kind of an error message. A few calculators will even claim that the result is 'infinity', which is a misuse of the idea of a limit by a programmer[*]. The reference to 'impossible' creates an impression that it could become possible one day. After all, subtracting 5 from 2 was 'impossible' before the introduction of negative numbers, and dividing 5 by 2 was impossible before introducing fractions. 'Not allowed' is the most problematic reference, however. Who doesn't allow it? What's the penalty? Many things that are 'not allowed' are still possible, like parking in a no-parking zone or smoking in a 'no smoking' area. 'Not allowed' is a particularly problematic term with school children, since teachers do not allow so many things, like talking to a friend, chewing gum, running in the hallway, submitting homework assignment after the deadline, etc. Is division by zero one of these teacher-invented and administration-supported rules? Is it still possible to do something not allowed if you are not caught?

As difficult as this is to untangle, a story can do just that. Let's start with a dead king, and his last will and testament. This will states that his 12 diamonds are to be divided equally among his living offspring. Now, let's say there are 6 offspring. (A grandma with 12 cookies and 6 grandchildren who come to visit can be a good substitute for a dead king and his heirs.) Not much convincing is needed to see that each heir gets 2 diamonds, and 2 is obtained by 12÷6. But before varying the story, let's focus on these 2 diamonds. To what question is "2 diamonds" the answer? The question is "how many diamonds will each heir get?" Having established that, let's vary our story.

Suppose there are only 4 heirs. Why four and not six? This is up to the creativity and imagination of the story teller. Maybe 2 of the heirs died in avalanche. Maybe the oldest brother, the firstborn, was extremely unhappy with the idea of equal sharing of inheritance and believed that he, as the firstborn, should get a lion's share of his father's treasure, if not all of it. So he found ways to slip poison into the drinks of his siblings, and so far was successful in killing two of his brothers. Whatever route is chosen, the facts reduce the number of heirs from 6 to 4. Now, how many diamonds will each heir get? Again, we get the answer of 3 by dividing the number of diamonds (12) by the number of heirs (4). And the story continues.

In a spirit of involving the audience in the story, we ask students to suggest what happens to another heir. Was it a car accident? Was it a stroke? An alien abduction? Was she so saddened by the king's death that she died from crying? Often students' suggestions are tied to current events, such as hurricanes, terrorist attacks, or stingray stabs to the heart. No agreement is necessary on this series of unfortunate events, but agreement on the fact that once there are 3 heirs, each gets 4 diamonds is essential and easily reached. Let us reiterate that the operation 12÷3 is performed to answer the question, "how many diamond does each heir get?"

---

[*] The result of division by zero is not infinity. However, the limit of the sequence a/x, for a positive real a and where x approaches zero from the positive side, is infinity.

Similarly, if there were 2 heirs each one would get 6 diamonds. And if the king had only one living child, that child would get all 12 of the diamonds, as 12÷1 = 12.

So far nothing unusual from a mathematical point of view has been described. But now the stage is set. It is time for the tragic conclusion to our story. The king's last remaining son has died in a plane crash on his way to attend his father's funeral. There are now zero heirs. At this point the will is unclear, and so is the mathematics. There are still 12 diamonds but we can no longer answer the question "how many diamonds will each heir get". We cannot answer "how many cookies will each grandchild get" if no grandchild comes to visit grandma. So the diamonds will go to the crown, grandma will eat the cookies herself or share with a neighbour; our questions will remain unanswerable and division by zero *undefined*.

We believe that recalling this story, or a similar one, will clarify the troublesome issue of division by zero and also reduce the confusion between division by zero and division of zero by another number. Of course, a story is not the only way to explain this concept. In what follows we present additional explanation, building on the human sense of patterns and relationships. Which explanation is better? Not only is beauty in the eye of a beholder, but so is utility and perceived explanatory power. Therefore we recommend the Russian artillery strategy: shoot many times, shoot many places, and hope that eventually somewhere and sometime a hit will be scored.

As usual, we start with something familiar and gradually proceed towards the goal. We start with highlighting a familiar relationship between multiplication and division.

Let's fill in the blanks:

$12 \div 3 =$ ___ → $\underline{4} \times 3 = 12$
$10 \div 5 =$ ___ → $\underline{2} \times 5 = 10$
$24 \div 8 =$ ___ → $\underline{3} \times 8 = 24$

For the first one, we look for a number that when multiplied by 3 will result in 12. That is, we ask, 3 multiplied by what equals 12? The answer is 4 and this is the result for 12 ÷ 3.

This result is derived from understanding the relationship between multiplication and division. With students, a handful of examples should be approached in a similar way, before attempting to fill in the blank for

$18 \div 0 =$ ___ → $\underline{?} \times 0 = 18$

Following the pattern in the examples above, we ask, what number multiplied by 0 will give us 18? This number will be the quotient in division of 18 by 0. But there is no such number. There is no possibility to define division by zero to keep it consistent with multiplication. Therefore, yet again, we leave it *undefined*.

In the spirit of Russian artillery referred to above, which can make a story of its own, we present yet another explanation, the one that connects division with

CHAPTER 7

repeated subtraction. It is a common practice to introduce multiplication as repeated addition. However, division is usually introduced and thought of as an inverse operation for multiplication. Alternatively, we can think of division as repeated subtraction. Consider for example 28÷7=4. In terms of partitive division (discussed above), we can think of 28 items placed in 7 equal sets. Alternatively, in terms of quotitive or measurement division, we can think of making sets of 7 items, and asking how many sets there are. A possible modelling approach for this situation is continuously removing sets of 7 items from the initial 28, or 'measuring' 28 with the units of 7. To calculate 28÷7, we ask, how many sevens can we remove from 28, until there is nothing left? Numerically this corresponds to $28 - 7 - 7 - 7 - 7 = 0$. So there are four sevens.

Let us reiterate the idea with another numerical example, say 15÷3. We can interpret this as how many threes can we remove from 15 to get zero? We need 5 threes, as $15 - 3 - 3 - 3 - 3 - 3 = 0$

Let us be very careful with the wording here. A common tendency is to ask, "How many times can you subtract 3 from 15?" A joking answer is: "You can subtract it as many times as you wish, if you do it correctly you will get 12 each time".

Jokes aside – as we devote a special chapter to them – we direct our discussion towards division by zero. In order to get the answer for 15÷0, we ask, how many zeros can you remove from 15 (or any other number) to get a zero?
$15 - 0 - 0 - 0 - 0 - 0 - 0 - 0 - 0 - 0 - 0$ ... ???

Yet again, this question of "how many" has no answer, which leaves division by zero as undefined.

Multiplication of negative numbers and changing temperatures

Multiplication of negative numbers is another mystery that teachers often find difficult to explain. "A negative times a negative equals a positive" is sometimes introduced as a 'rule to follow'. Obviously, following such rules is not such a bad principle to live by. It will, more often than not, lead to a correct solution and all the praise that comes with it. As mentioned, however, our mission here is not to recite the rules, but to explain the logic behind them. While addition of integers is nicely modeled using a number line, multiplication is more of a challenge.

A common explanation for multiplication of integers relies on patterns. Consider, for example, the pattern in multiplication by 3:

$$4 \times 3 = 12$$
$$3 \times 3 = 9$$
$$2 \times 3 = 6$$
$$1 \times 3 = 3$$
$$0 \times 3 = 0$$
$$-1 \times 3 = \underline{}$$
$$-2 \times 3 = \underline{}$$

With a strong sense of pattern – that we believe students acquire from exploring the multiplication tables prior to being exposed to operations with negative numbers – students observe that the left column decreases by 1, the middle column is constant and the right column decreases by 3. Following this pattern the next entries on the right will be (-3) and (-6). This may be sufficient to establish a general rule that "a negative times a positive is a negative". Once this is established, a similar strategy can be applied for "a negative times a negative".

$$4 \times (-3) = -12$$
$$3 \times (-3) = -9$$
$$2 \times (-3) = -6$$
$$1 \times (-3) = -3$$
$$0 \times (-3) = 0$$
$$-1 \times (-3) = \underline{}$$
$$-2 \times (-3) = \underline{}$$

While the numbers on the left decrease by 1, and the middle is constant, the numbers on the right increase by 3. Keeping with the sequence, the next entries are 3 and 6 and so on, exemplifying or convincing that – as unusual as it may appear at first – the product of two negative numbers is positive.

While patterns may be convincing by instilling or reinforcing the feeling of regularity and stability, they do little in order to *explain* the situation. This is why we turn to a story, a story that explains.

As usually, we start with a familiar situation. We consider a chemical reaction, in which the temperature is rising by 2 degrees every hour. The current temperature is 0. What will the temperature be in 5 hours? This situation can be modelled by multiplication, $2 \times 5 = 10$, where the answer of 10 degrees represents the temperature in 5 hours. In this case both factors are positive. The temperature is rising and the hourly rise is given by (positive) 2. The time line moves into the future, and the moment 'in 5 hours' is represented by (positive) 5. In varying the story, either of these attributes can become negative. First we vary each one of them separately, and then consider both variations at the same time.

Variation 1:
Consider a chemical reaction in which the temperature is *decreasing* by 2 degrees every hour. The current temperature is 0. What will the temperature be in 5 hours? It is natural to represent the hourly decrease in a temperature by (-2). In this case the situation is modelled by $(-2) \times 5 = (-10)$.

Variation 2:
Consider a chemical reaction in which temperature is *increasing* by 2 degrees every hour. The current temperature is 0. What was the temperature 5 hours ago? Here we are moving in the negative direction on the timeline. Where 5 represents

CHAPTER 7

the point in time to happen 'in 5 hours', it makes sense to use (-5) to represent the point in time of '5 hours ago'. Then, the situation is modelled by 2 × (-5) = (-10).

Variation 3:
Consider a chemical reaction in which the temperature is *decreasing* by 2 degrees every hour. The current temperature is 0. What was the temperature 5 hours ago? Clearly, the temperature 5 hours ago was 10 degrees, as from that point it reached 0 in 5 steps of 2. However, in consistency with previously established representations, the current situation is represented by (-2) × (-5). Putting these two conclusions together, we get (-2) × (-5) = 10. This, of course, is consistent with the 'rule', and if used correctly it achieves more than just a correct answer.

Numerical variation

The three examples explored above have several things in common. First, they deal with ideas that are known to be problematic for learners. Then, as expected, they attempt to explain the difficulty with a story. But there is a similarity within the stories themselves. What we called here a story is not a structured sequence of events that has a beginning, a middle, and an end. Instead, it is a description of a situation, an ever changing situation, or, alternatively a variable story. We start with a simple unproblematic scenario. Then we change the numbers, repeating the change several times. Gradual variations with compatible numbers help in establishing a general mathematical template, an operation, or a pattern. Once the general structure is recognized, it stays invariant when 'problematic' numbers – fractions, zero, negative numbers – are introduced. However, as the numerical variation is gradual, the 'problematic' numbers fit the generated template naturally and the desired relationship is established.

Changing stories by changing numbers can help not only with problematic ideas, but in solving a variety of problems. In the next section we show how numerical variation – that is, changing numbers in the tasks while keeping the structure invariant – is a helpful strategy on a pathway to a solution.

CHANGING STORIES TO CLARIFY CONFUSION

To exemplify numerical variation as a means towards generality we consider two classic puzzles and two rather conventional, but troublesome problems.

On chickens, eggs and grain

Consider the following well known riddle:
> *If a hen-and-a-half lays an egg-and-a-half in a day-and-a-half, how many days does it take one hen to lay one egg?*

Many students either answer 'one day' by inertia or claim that the problem presents impossible nonsense. Only a very few students suppress these tendencies and attempt to reason their way through the available information. What does this twist on a chicken and an egg problem have to do with anything? We believe that by the end of this section the connection will become clear. However, let us consider first a more 'realistic' problem.

A pound of grain cost $1.68. How much grain can you buy for $0.50?

Fair enough, this is not a story. One may even say that it is a 'standard' textbook problem. However, we can easily turn it into a story. There could be a dragon and a prince. And the grain can be a love potion. Or, there could be a poor boy that needs cup of this 'special' grain to cure his grandma of a terrible disease. So he finds a magic farmer who grows this grain and is ready to sell it to our hero for $1.68 per pound. But the boy, our hero, only has $.50 in his pocket. As we show in the next chapter, any standard textbook problem can be presented as a story. But now let us turn to the mathematics the problem invites.

We presented this problem to various populations, from middle school students to prospective elementary school teachers, and a significant number of people made errors in setting up the division statement, that is, dividing 1.68 by 0.50 rather than 0.50 by 1.68. What is the best way to help them? Of course, pointing to their error is not helpful beyond the given problem.

The general multiplicative structure that a learner needs to recognize in order to solve this problem is: A pound of grain costs X. How much grain can you buy for Y? This is an example of a more general form of quotitive (measurement) division, that is, a division structure that determines how many times X can fit into Y, or how Y can be measured by X. This structure is problematic, as we alerted above in discussing division by a fraction.

Once the structure is recognized, the solution is given by Y÷X. The question, however, is what is it that can guide learners towards seeing the generality in this particular case (Mason & Pimm, 1984)? What we found helpful is changing the numbers.

A pound of grain cost $2. How much grain can you buy for $6?

A pound of grain cost $2. How much grain can you buy for $20?

The numbers in these examples are compatible, that is, easily manipulated and work well together. Learners seldom have problems with these kinds of questions, so using them as a starting point is beneficial. Once the general structure is established, it is possible to move to 'more problematic' numbers, involving fractions.

A pound of grain cost $2. How much grain can you buy for $0.50?

And then gradually return to the original problem. Will the grandma survive?

This strategy can be seen as a modification of the "structured variation grids" (Mason, 2001, 2007) in that it is a gradual numerical variation for the purpose of prompting recognition of structure. So, why is the structure more readily recognized when numbers are compatible than when they are not? We suggest that the source of the obstacle is with the perceived range of permissible change. That is, the numbers in the initial problem are 'too far' from the students' example space

CHAPTER 7

of problems that are associated, implicitly, with measurement division. Numerical variation assists in recognizing similarities and extending the general structure, a step necessary for the solution.

Now we return to the infamous chickens and eggs.

If 6 hens lay 6 eggs in one day, how long will it take one hen to lay one egg?

This wording may suggest keeping 'one chicken' as invariant and ask further:

If 6 hens lay 6 eggs in a day and a half, how long will it take one hen to lay one egg?

Or

If 6 hens lay 6 eggs in 6 days, how long will it take one hen to lay one egg?

This apparent analogy to the initial problem suggests a pathway towards a solution. However, in our experience the problem may still present a challenge to many learners.

On 'big' percentages

We often smile when someone claims to be putting 120% of his energy in a project or being 200% sure of something. These claims exemplify a tendency to overemphasize an effort or certainty, rather than provide an accurate measure. When a whole is 100%, what is indicated by a percentage higher than 100? We found that when a high percentage appears in a mathematical problem situation it often leads the learners away from recognizing the general structure. Consider for example the following problem:

The price of a can of coffee was $10. It increased by 400%, what is the new price?

In a class of prospective elementary school teachers, about half of the students claimed that the new price was $40, explaining that 400% meant 'quadrupling'. Once again, what we found helpful towards recognizing the general strategy is numerical variation:

The price of a can of coffee was $10. It increased by 20%, what is the new price?

The price of a can of coffee was $10. It increased by 35%, what is the new price?

The price of a can of coffee was $10. It increased by 100%, what is the price now?

Again, we believe that the main problem is with the perceived range of permissible change. While 20%, 35%, or even 100% fits within what is expected – both in a real world context and in a mathematics classroom context – the increase of 400% appears beyond a 'reasonable' permissible change. These numbers, or similar numbers, can be used progressively in a story about outrageous inflation or price

STORIES THAT EXPLAIN

gouging. Perhaps the story is about a class fieldtrip to a disreputable amusement park where the park owners raise the price of bottled water as the day gets hotter and the trip is scheduled on the hottest day of the year. Or maybe we are talking about a super drink that increases strength and endurance. Regardless, of the story the progressive use of these numbers can help students bridge their understanding of percentages to situations such as a 400% increase. We now turn to another popular riddle, and attempt to explain it with numerical variation.

Missing dollar

The 'missing dollar riddle' or 'missing dollar paradox' is a famous puzzle that appears in many published collections of mathematical problems. The riddle begins with the story of three men who check into a hotel. The cost of their room, they are told, is $30. So, they each contribute $10 and go upstairs. Later the manager realizes that he has overcharged the men and that the actual cost should have been only $25. The manager promptly sends the bellboy upstairs to return the extra $5 to the men. The bellboy, however, decides to cheat the men and pockets $2 for himself and returns $1 to each of the men. As a result, each man has now paid $9 to stay in the room (3 × $9 = $27) and the bellboy has pocketed $2 ($27 + $2 = $29). The men initially paid $30, so the question is, *where is the missing dollar?*

Another version of this story changes the scene and the players, but keeps the numbers constant. Three ladies go to a restaurant for a meal. They receive a bill for $30. They each put $10 on the table, which the waiter collects and takes to the till. The cashier informs the waiter that the bill should only have been for $25 and returns $5 to the waiter in $1 coins. On the way back to the table the waiter realizes that he cannot divide the coins equally between the ladies. As they didn't know the total of the revised bill, he decides to put $2 in his own pocket and give each of the ladies $1. Now that each lady has been given a dollar back, they have each paid $9. Three times $9 is $27. The waiter has $2 in his pocket. $2 plus $27 is $29. The ladies originally handed over $30. Where is the missing dollar?

Although the setting and the characters have changed, what has not changed is the numbers – and the numbers are problematic in their compatibility. That is to say, the incorrect calculation ($29) brings us very close to the given initial value ($30), and that is where the problem, and the perceived paradox, lies. A variety of experts on a variety of websites and forum discussions have tried to explain the miscalculation. We would like to clarify it as well. However, unlike other explanations, which stay with the story, we alter the story by implementing a numerical change. The paradox in the aforementioned situations is created by adding the $2 pocketed by the waiter or the bellboy to the $27 paid by the ladies or the men. Adding these two amounts does not answer any question. However, subtracting 2 from the 27 answers the question of how much was actually received as payment by the cashier or the receptionist at the hotel desk.

It is clear that the above explanation, or others similar to it, do not 'work'. People are still puzzled with the difference between the $29 that the story mentions and the desired initial $30, and so the search for the missing dollar continues. This

CHAPTER 7

is why the puzzle has survived for so many generations and, we suspect, will continue to intrigue curious minds for many generations to come. For those who strive to understand, however, we offer a different story – one that is actually the same story but with different numbers. Let us say that the actual room cost was only $20, and the bellboy was sent to return $10 to the men. For simplicity of division, he pocketed $1 and returned $3 to each of the men. In this situation the men paid $7 each, for the total of $21. The bellboy has $1. Adding the actual payment to the one pocketed dollar gives us $22. Would it make sense to suggest, starting with the initial collection of $30, that $8 are missing? And if this is not convincing enough, let us change the numbers in the story once again, giving the men a "Stay with us for 1/3 the price" coupon, and send the bellboy to return to them $20. By now, knowing the bellboy's desire for a simple and fair division, we have him pocket $2 and return $18 to the men, $6 each. In this situation the men paid $4 each, for a total of $12. The bellboy has $2. Adding the actual payment to the two pocketed dollars gives us $14. Would it make sense to suggest, starting with the initial collection of $30, that $16 are missing?

We noticed that varying numbers, whether large or small, helps in making sense of the situation. Numerical variation in the story could be more convincing than any attempts to explain the original one. The absurdity of the missing dollar in the original situation is brought to the surface when we establish the general structure of adding the paid amount to the pocketed amount. If the general structure of 'missing money' makes no sense, neither does its specific example of the 'missing dollar'.

Mixing wine and water, a discrete variation

Another famous mathematical problem, often presented as a puzzle, gives a scenario of two identical glasses, one filled with water, and another filled with the same amount of wine. Then, for no other reason but to create a problem, a spoon of wine is poured into water, and a spoon from a water-with-wine mixture is poured back into the glass of wine. Now, the question is, is there more wine in the water or more water in the wine? Of course, those who do not like to spoil wine with water and those who prefer to stay away from alcohol may present the problem with a different choice of liquids. A popular variation considers two jars of paint, say red and blue. For a reader unfamiliar with the problem we suggest that you put the book aside and try to solve it.

The solution – that the amount of water in wine is the same as the amount of wine in water – comes as a surprise to many, and the algebraic manipulation that clearly suggests the answer appears counterintuitive. We suggest a variation – not to prove the outcome, we believe algebra does it well – to regain the intuition.

Suppose that, rather than a problem of glasses of water and wine or two jars of paint, we tell a story about two buses, one red and one blue. On a red bus there are 10 girls and on a blue bus there are 10 boys. They are travelling to a specific event chosen for a specific reason, depending on the imagination of the story teller. Both buses stop for a break and at some point 3 girls go and visit the boys in their blue bus. Then, there is a sudden call for the buses to leave (we let the imagination of the story teller create both the need for the girls' visit and the emergency situation that requires a sudden departure). Leaving in a hurry – and just because each bus can carry only 10 passengers – 3 kids from the blue bus run and take seats in the red bus. So, which number is bigger, boys on the red bus or girls on the blue bus?

The answer will depend, of course, on the 3 kids who ran from the blue bus to the red. If all 3 were girls, we are back to the initial sitting – there are no girls on the blue bus and no boys on the red bus. If all 3 were boys – we have 3 boys on the red bus and 3 girls on the red bus. If there are 2 girls and 1 boy we will have as a result 1 boy coming over to the red bus and 1 girl remaining on the blue bus. Similarily, if there are 2 boys and 1 girl running over from the blue bus, we will have 2 boys on the red bus and 2 girls remaining on the blue bus. Whatever the combination is, the answer does not change: the number of boys on the red bus is the same as the number of girls on the blue bus. The sceptics – as well as the students – are invited to check other possibilities. What if the number of kids on each bus was 20 or 50 rather than 10? What if the number of 'initial visitors' was 2, or 5 or 10, rather than 3?

Mixing wine and water may be different from mixing boys and girls. However, we hope that simple numerical analogue of a story is helpful in making sense of the original continuous situation.

Changing the context – Supermarket dollar exchange

In previous examples we discussed numerical variation, that is, changing the numbers. In this section we will focus on changing the context.

This is a true story. Many stories we tell as if it happened to one of us. But this one really did happen to one of us. That is why the story is told in the first person.

> *One day I entered a large supermarket downtown to get some groceries. I do not usually shop there, but it was on my way, and I needed only a few things. When I was at the cashier, I noticed a sign that said "US dollar exchange: 27%". I pondered for a moment, what does this mean? I was in the mood of educating the world and instilling numeracy in every citizen, and so I tried to explain to the cashier that the sign did not make much sense, and the proper way would be to say $1 US = $1.27 CAD. The cashier gave me this "are you stupid, or what?" look. She claimed that everyone but me understood exactly what the sign meant, that she made quite a few exchanges that day, and the days before that, and no one ever got confused or complained. No one but me, of course.*

> *I didn't give up. I went to talk to the manager, a nice middle-aged man with a French accent. I explained, to the best of my ability, that the sign could be interpreted in several possible ways, and offered a correct way to post the exchange rate. The manager immediately asked whether I was a mathematician, and he seemed to understand my point. He even thanked me for noticing, and for my concern, and promised to change the sign. I walked*

CHAPTER 7

out in a good mood, feeling respected and believing that I made the world a better place, or at least a more 'numerate' place. A few days later I visited the same supermarket. The sign was indeed changed. Now it said "US dollar exchange: 28%".

This story was shared with some of our students who were prospective teachers. They didn't seem impressed. After all, everyone knows how to convert money, they claimed, especially how to convert an American dollar to a Canadian dollar. So in order to make a point, we told another story. Suppose, the students were told, that you have been chosen to go to Mars as a part of your teacher education program. Student exchange programs are getting rather popular, so while other groups may be going to Mexico or England, your destination is Mars. In order to prepare for the trip, you want to exchange your Canadian dollars to Martian dollars. You are told: "Martian dollar exchange: 37%". What amount, in Martian dollars, will you get for $100 CAD?

The answers varied. Some claimed this would be $37 (taking 37% of 100), others suggested it should be $137 (adding 37% to the amount) or $63 (subtracting 37% from the amount). Changing the context, presenting the case in which there was no prior knowledge to make sense of the situation, helped in making the point, and helped in supporting the claim that the information was not well-defined.

Unlike the stories discussed previously, a variation presented here served in creating the confusion, rather than clarifying the confusion. However, the presented confusion made it clear that the information was not presented properly, and hopefully, raised the awareness of possible misinterpretations and the need for clarity.

SUMMARY

We presented here stories or problem situations that address several mathematical ideas that are known to be difficult to explain by teachers and difficult to understand by students. The common feature in all these stories, from the perspective of storytelling, is the notion of repetition or repetition with variation. It is not from her first try that Goldilocks finds the most comfortable chair or the porridge that is just right. It is not from the first trial that the Prince finds a girl who can wear a shoe lost by Cinderella. A search, repetition with variation, is what brings ultimate success. The same is sometimes true when it comes to understanding mathematics.

The common feature in these stories, from the perspective of mathematics, is that they refer to a very simple and very familiar situation and then gradually explore variations of it until the otherwise problematic situation is arrived at. Rather than strange facts to be memorized and strange rules to be obeyed, this gradual exposure by varying certain elements in a story presents mathematical rules and facts as logical extensions of, or derivations from, prior knowledge,

Numerical variation is recognized in instruction as a viable strategy. We have shown how it can be implemented starting with small or compatible numbers and then, once the structure is established, moved towards larger or stranger numbers.

We have also considered the benefits of numerical variation in the 'opposite direction', that is, starting with a confusing situation and then varying the numbers in order to reveal the underlying general structure. Such an approach is analogous to the "consider simpler but similar problem" heuristic suggested by Polya (1945/1988). In the same way that simpler but similar variations of a given problem help reach a solution, simpler but similar variations of a scenario in a story help with the understanding of difficult concepts or counterintuitive results. We have also shown how changing the context of a story – to a similar, but not necessarily a simpler problem – can help in directing students' attention to mathematics.

CHAPTER 8

STORIES THAT ASK A QUESTION

Mathematics textbooks often consist of many so-called 'exercises' and 'problems'. What are referred to as exercises, in this context, are strings of calculations, used to drill and practice and reinforce learned methods or algorithms. What are called problems are actually not much different in purpose, but quite different in form. Problems are written with words rather than symbols and solving them usually involves a coordinated effort to decode these words into a number sentence followed by the correct application of the correct algorithm to arrive at the final solution. For example, while 3+5 is seen as an exercise, in a typical problem this exercise would be encoded to include Jack and Jill and the combining of some marbles. In textbooks such problems usually appear towards the end of a chapter or a section and are predicated on the most recently learned algorithms.

What are often called 'problems', in reference to mathematics in school, are very different from the idea of 'problem solving' as an introduction to mathematical activity. The standard notion of a *mathematical problem*, as used in mathematics education literature, refers to a task for which no algorithm or a standard approach is immediately obvious. As such, what can be called a problem is dependent on the knowledge and prior experiences of learners.

As distinguished from 'real' mathematical problems, school problems are often referred to as word-problems or story-problems. In fact, they are skeletons of stories that got stripped of their engaging details. We discuss here how the story can be reintroduced into some traditional word problems.

DRESSING UP

The following story can be used not only to introduce a mathematical idea but also to extend it. We first present a word problem. Then we show how the problem can be turned into a story, making a mathematical activity more engaging.

Problem (conventional wording):
>If set A has 3 elements and set B has 4 elements, how many elements are there in a Cartesian product A×B?

With a bit less 'pompous' terminology, the same problem can be worded as follows:
>Set A has 3 elements and set B has 4 elements. Your task is to create a set C, the elements of which are all the possible ordered pairs, where the first element in the pair is from set A and the second element in the pair is from set B. How many pairs are there in C?

CHAPTER 8

This problem can also be presented as a story. A variation on this wording can be found in many elementary textbooks.

Problem as a story:
>Kathy has 3 skirts and 4 blouses. How many possible outfits can she make (assuming that each skirt can go with each blouse and an outfit consists of a skirt and a blouse)?

But *telling* a story requires further elaboration. In Chapter 3 we exemplified several elements of telling as well as of involving students in story-telling. The following is an additional example of involving students in a problem via telling a story, using some humorous undertones. Without loss of generality, we have chosen to present this telling of a story in a female voice.

>*I was a few minutes late for class today. Did you notice? No? I would like to share with you why I was late. My alarm woke me up at the usual time, I had breakfast at my usual time, and I started to get dressed at my usual time. But when I opened my closet I was faced with a dilemma. There were 3 skirts and 4 blouses hanging there, and I couldn't make up my mind. There was a black skirt, a navy skirt and a green skirt. And the 4 blouses were white, pink, red and yellow. Maybe I should choose a black skirt with a white blouse? Or maybe a green skirt with a pink blouse? What would you suggest? (wait) You see, you can't decide. I couldn't decide either. That's why I was late for class. Do you know how many different outfits I had to consider?*

Here, of course, is a pause to give students time to consider the question as well as an opportunity to come up with an answer. For very young students the activity may involve actual colouring of the outfit. For older ones the usual strategy is to introduce some symbolic coding and list the possibilities. Based on the age and mathematical sophistication of students, such symbolic coding may note the specific colours, for example using SB, SN and SG to denote black, navy, and green skirts respectively, or may acknowledge the number of objects, rather than their specific colours, for example using S1, S2, S3 to distinguish between the three skirt and B1, B2, B3 and B4 to distinguish between the three blouses. A systematic listing will acknowledge the following combinations:

S1-B1	S2-B1	S3-B1
S1-B2	S2-B2	S3-B2
S1-B3	S2-B3	S3-B3
S1-B4	S2-B4	S3-B4

For many, such an exhaustive and systematic listing may suffice. However, here is an opportunity to extend the story in order to introduce an important mathematical idea.

>*Let's now say that my jacket is also a part of my outfit, and that I had 2 jackets. How many different outfits will I have to consider now?*

STORIES THAT ASK A QUESTION

> *And of course I will not come to class without shoes. Suppose I also have 12 pairs of shoes. So each outfit consists of a shirt, a blouse, a jacket and a pair of shoes. How many outfits would I have to consider in this case?*

Note the choice of numbers. The original story and the first extension can simply be solved by making lists, a strategy that is sometimes referred to as "exhaustive counting" – a method of "systematically accounting of all the possibilities". It is also not hard to extend the initial list of 12 to the list of 24, including jackets in the outfit. However, the choice of a 'large' number in the next step invites generalization.

Staying with the story, students are invited to consider the addition of a hat to the outfit, knowing that there are 37 possible hats. The improbability of this large number raises many smiles. A joke? Of course. But a joke with a purpose in that the obvious exaggeration of this number tells the students that the teacher is now expecting them to find the general treatment of this type of problem. We further invite students to extend the story by adding more items to the outfit – socks, scarves, gloves, jewellery, glasses, etc. Another variation is to constrain the story:

> *Suppose I had slacks as well, 5 pairs. But I wouldn't wear slacks and a skirt. How would this change the number of outfits?*

Building on this experience, students conclude that a solution is given by multiplying the numbers that show how many items there are in each component of the outfit. Using mathematical language, the solution is given by the product of the number of elements in each set. Formalizing further, a general strategy can be derived; whenever we have to make successive choices, the total number of possibilities is the product of the numbers indicating the number of choices in each step.

And a teacher's narrative may continue as follows:

> *This property is so important in mathematics, that it was given a big name. It is called the fundamental principle of counting. Yes,* **The Fundamental Principle of Counting.** *(Capital letters and bold font here indicate raising a voice). But if you forget this name, you may simply call it "My teacher's morning dilemma".*

We would like to call the reader's attention, yet again, to the notion of *telling*. In our case this is not simple artistic telling, but an interactive telling. The teacher provides the frame, but the students become participants in the telling by deciding how to extend the story by choosing additional items to add to the outfit. Thus, we move from a rather simple situation, that can be explored with very young students, to a generalized theorem, rather useful in a variety of mathematical problems.

... FOR A PARTY

Having considered all the possible outfits, and hopefully having chosen an appropriate one for a party, let us consider a story of a meeting at a party, usually referred to as a 'handshakes problem'.

CHAPTER 8

> *Last night we had a party. A very nice one. The DJ played 107 different songs. The bar had 7 choices of cocktails. For dinner there were 4 different appetizers including chopped liver and lobster tail salad.*

Maybe we could have continued this description and asked for the number of possible dinner combinations, composed of a cocktail, an appetizer and a song. But the focus we have chosen this time is on welcoming and introducing the guests.

> *As the guests arrived, every person shook hands with all the other guests...*

How many handshakes were there? – is the usual question. The answer, of course, will depend on the number of people who arrived at the party. In a traditional goal-oriented classroom this question can be preceded just with one sentence: "There were (whatever number you want) people and everyone shook hands with everyone else." However, in our case, a story about a party precedes the question.

What is gained by turning this rather standard problem into a story? For some students this could be an attention-getting tool, a story to remember and to associate with problems involving combinations. From the instructional perspective this is an opportunity to act it out in several ways, starting with the host and having the guests arrive one by one, recording the results, or, alternatively, having all the guests present and arranged in a circle and then exploring efficient possibilities for counting their handshakes.

Such a telling leads to another valuable element of story-telling that has surfaced in the two stories presented in this chapter. This element is personalization. In both – the story of choosing outfits and the story of a party and handshakes – the teacher tells a story about herself/himself, rather than about Little Red Riding Hood, Gauss, or Quint. As a result, when the story starts, the students have no idea that it is a deliberate and planned part of a lesson.

STUDENTS AS PROBLEM ACTORS: KING SOLOMON AND QUEEN SHEBA

We have already mentioned possible ways to involve students in a story, such as telling and retelling repetitive parts, choosing names for characters, or determining the next set of actions. We have also mentioned the importance of having students relate to the protagonist in the story, where the best character to identify with is the one who resembles the students themselves. This may explain the success of Harry Potter. We also just mentioned a possible benefit of making the storyteller one of the actors in the story, by telling a story about him/herself. Another possible strategy to enhance students' engagement is in making the students themselves the heroes or the actors.

Recall the example of Amzula the shepherd who didn't know how to count. How was he to ensure that all the sheep that left in the morning returned in the evening? We turn this question over to students, but in addition to the question itself, we also introduce role playing. Rather than saying "how could the shepherd figure this out", we say, "pretend that you are the shepherd, what would you do?" And then students can present their ideas referring to what *they would have done* rather than what *could be* done in general. In our experience, this minor twist in a question makes students not only more engaged with the task but also more responsible in reporting their suggestions. It gives them ownership of the problem and also ownership of the solution. That it to say, the problem is *theirs*, rather than Amzula's, the prince's, or Oedipus'. It is theirs to face and theirs to solve. We present here the first of three examples of this kind of student engagement.

King Solomon is known to be the wisest of men. A well known story from the Bible talks about him settling a bitter dispute between two harlots, each claiming to be the mother of a newborn baby. King Solomon suggested slicing the baby in half. One woman agreed whereas the other offered to give up the child and save his life. Such a generous offer could have come only from the real mother, and that one was indeed awarded the child.

A much less known story is about King Solomon and Queen Sheba, whom Solomon desperately wanted to marry, despite having remarkable success with many other women.

> *Upon Solomon's marriage proposal, Queen Sheba asked the servants to bring two identical bowls, one with 10 silver talents, the other with 10 gold ones. She suggested that Solomon be blindfolded and then chose only one bowl and one talent from that bowl. "If you chose the gold talent, I will marry you" – Sheba said to Solomon.*
>
> *The King considered his odds for a moment, and then asked whether he would be permitted to rearrange the talents in the two bowls before making his blindfolded choice. Sheba was surprised with the request. With ten gold talents in one bowl, and 10 silver talents in the other bowl, she knew that the chance of drawing the gold talent was ½. Suppose, she thought, the talents were mixed and each bowl held 5 gold ones and 5 silver ones, she could not see how this might change the situation. But should she grant King Solomon's request?*

We stop here and turn to students: "Suppose you were Queen Sheba. Would you grant Solomon's request? Why or why not?" "Suppose you were King Solomon. Why would you want to rearrange the talents? Could this make any difference?"

Solomon's request appears unusual because the initial assumption people make is that rearranging the talents will still result in equal amounts in each bowl. This indeed, will not change the chances of choosing the gold one. However, the twist is that when the numbers in the bowls are different the chances change significantly. The best scenario – and indeed the one that the King may have proposed – is to leave just one gold talent in one of the bowls and put the remaining 9 gold talents and 10 silver talents in the other bowl. The exact calculation, and exploring different arrangements of talents, may serve as an introduction to conditional probability in the higher grades. However, even for elementary students it is easy to see that with this proposed arrangement, if Solomon chooses the bowl with the one gold talent then it is 100% certain that he will chose the gold one, and if his initial choice is for the mixed bowl, the chance of drawing the gold talent is 9/19, which is a bit over 47% and very close to ½. As such, the total chance is very close to ¾. So, by rearranging the talents, the chances of marrying Queen Sheba have been enhanced significantly. Further, by putting students 'in the shoes' of the King and the Queen the likelihood that the students will find ways to increase (or decrease) the chances of marriage has been enhanced.

And – likely with the help of the gold talent – history tells us that Solomon did marry Sheba and they had a son who became the first king of Ethiopia.

STUDENTS AS PROBLEM ACTORS: THE BEDOUIN WILL

This famous story is told in different variations. We shall try one of these here.

Once upon a time there was an old Bedouin who had three sons...

Maybe here is the time for cross curricular intervention: Who are the Bedouins? (Nomadic Arab tribes) Where do they live? (Middle East and North Africa) How do they travel? (Camels). Once the mode of transportation is established, the story may continue.

So, needless to say, camels are very important to the Bedouins. They serve them not only for travel and the transfer of goods from one place to another, but their skins make wonderful coats and rugs for the tents. Furthermore, the fact that the camel can store enough food and drink for several weeks makes it an ideal animal for travel in the desert. But, our story is not only about camels, but also about a very old Bedouin and his three sons.

And as it often happens to very old people, the old Bedouin died. And, as it often happens, not only among Bedouins, the Old Bedouin left his treasure to his sons, with explicit instructions for how the treasure was to be divided. And what was his main treasure? Camels, of course. So the Old Bedouin willed that his oldest son should get 1/2 of the camels, the middle son 1/3 of the camels and the younger son 1/9 of the camels. There were 17 camels left for the sons.

So the sons had a very difficult problem to solve. They couldn't cut the camels. They couldn't sell the camels and divide the money – this would be unthinkable in their tribe and considered disrespectful of their father's wishes. They thought and thought and thought... and could not agree upon a solution. So they decided to approach the wise elder of the tribe and seek advice. They looked for him all over and finally found him resting under the tree with his camel. The problem has no solution, the sons said, so we seek your advice on how to proceed.

This is the place to turn the story over to the students. Imagine, we put forward to students, that you are the wise elder of the tribe. What would you suggest to the sons? Students develop their suggestion and present them to the class. It is possible to accept all of them, or let the students choose the best one. It may be the case that some students will develop the same solution that was suggested by the wise elder.

No need to fight, he suggested. Take my camel and add it to your herd. This was thought to be overly generous and the son could not initially

> *comprehend the unexpected kindness. But the wise elder continued: Then the oldest brother should take 9 camels, which is 1/2 of 18, the middle son will get 6 camels, which is 1/3 of 18, and the youngest will get 2 camels, which is 1/9 of 18. And that way I will get back my dear camel and let it rest under the tree, as he is very tired after our last journey.*

The problem is solved, but the story does not end there. We then ask the students to consider whether the way of dividing the camels suggested by the wise elder and accepted by the sons is indeed in accordance with the will. After all, 9 out of 17 is not a half, and 6 out of 17 is not a third. The desirable conclusion in this discussion is that the will was 'illegal', as the sum of the parts does not result in a whole. To illustrate, one cannot will 1/2 of the estate to one son and 3/4 to the other, as the total results in more than the whole estate. In any case, the solution proposed by the wise elder was not in accord with the will, but the closest approximation, given the circumstances.

A similar story is described in the book *The Man Who Counted* by Malba Tahan (Tahan, 1972). There, two voyagers are travelling on the same camel and meet 3 brothers who face a dilemma similar to the sons of the Old Bedouin. Only in their case there are 35 camels that have to be divided as 1/2, 1/3 and 1/9. One of the travellers suggests solving the problem by adding their own camel to the pot to be divided. The other traveller is shocked, concerned that they will not be able to continue the journey without the camel. However, as the numbers turn out, the older son gets 18 camels, which is 1/2 of 36, the middle son gets 12 camels, which is 1/3 of the 36, and the youngest one gets 4 camels, which is 1/9 of 36. This makes for a total of 34 camels. Surprisingly or not, the travellers not only get back their own camel, but also get one from the herd, as a gift for their wise solution. So they continue their journey together, with each riding a different camel.

To further develop the understanding of the mathematical ideas in these stories the students can be asked to write their own 'camel stories'. The assignment is to vary the numbers, such that a similar story with a similar solution makes sense. Once several variations are presented, a generalization can be developed: What should the fractions in the story be in order to make a 'good' camel story? Once the imagination is triggered, students will vary not only the numbers, but also the scenery. After all, the mathematical activity is with fractions, not with camels.

THREE BEARS IN A DIFFERENT STORY

Everyone has heard the story of the three bears. There was papa-bear, mama-bear, and baby-bear. But this is a different story. There is no Goldilocks and no porridge. But there are apples and fairies. This is how the story goes:

> *Once upon a time there were three bears. But you already knew that. There should always be three bears in a story of three bears. But these weren't a papa-bear, a mama-bear, and a baby-bear. These were sibling-bears. Maybe triplets. Maybe brothers. Maybe two sisters and a brother. You*

CHAPTER 8

> *decide. You may also give them names. But until you chose other names. Let us call them Minnie, Mickey and Molly.*
>
> *So one sunny day the bears went for a walk in the forest. They played games, picked berries and enjoyed themselves. They lost all sense of time in their joyful games and were very surprised when it suddenly got dark. It got so dark that they could not find their way home. And so they wandered around until they became very tired and very hungry. They sat under a tree to get some rest, and ... they all fell asleep. At that time a kind fairy was passing by. She saw the three bears and thought that they looked hungry. So, she left them a basket of apples and continued on doing her good deeds in the forest. In the middle of the night Minnie, the oldest bear woke up. She saw a basket of tasty red apples and thought: "What a wonderful treat, these apples look so good and I'm so hungry. I want to eat them all". But then she remembered that she was not alone, and her siblings were likely hungry as well. She also remembered what mama-bear taught her children about sharing. So Minnie ate only one-third of the apples and immediately fell back to sleep.*
>
> *Another hour passed by and Mickey woke up. He saw a basket of tasty red apples and thought: "What a wonderful treat, these apples look so good and I'm so hungry. I want to eat them all". But then he remembered that he was not alone, and his siblings were likely hungry as well. He also remembered what mama-bear taught her children about sharing. So Mickey ate only one-third of the apples and immediately fell back to sleep.*
>
> *Another hour passed by and...*

Here it is appropriate to let one of the students to continue the story. The pattern is clear: each bear, in turn, eats one third of what is in the basket. And after Molly successfully falls asleep after eating her apples, we take charge of continuing the story.

> *Slowly, the forest awoke to the sunny morning. The birds were singing and their lovely songs woke the three sleeping bears. They saw a basket under the tree. What was in the basket?*

At this time we consider students' suggestions. Inevitably, some students suggest that the basket was empty, as each bear ate one-third of the apples. However, other students may object to this opinion, claiming that each ate only one-third of what was in the basket when she or he woke up. Thus, if Molly ate one-third of what was in the basket when she woke up, two thirds of this amount should still be in the basket. Only when this is agreed upon by the students is it time to pose a question. If there were 8 apples left in the basket when the bears awoke in the morning, how many apples did the Fairy leave them?

This story problem can be presented to elementary school students and to prospective teachers. In our experience, teachers who are trying to use algebra to find the solution are usually not successful. Using a strategy of working backwards or drawing diagrams brings the solution forward faster and in a more convincing manner. In the morning there were 8 apples. This is 2/3 of what Molly saw when she woke up. So, there were 12 apples in the basket at that time. 12 apples is 2/3 of what Mickey saw when woke up. So, there were 18 apples in the basket at that time. Finally, 18 apples are 2/3 of what Minnie saw, and of what the Fairy left. So, in the beginning there were 27 apples in the basket.

However, the solution itself is not our main interest here. What is most important is that this story introduces, in a powerful and playful way, the idea that a fraction is related to the initial amount taken as a whole, and that this whole may change.

Lack of attention to the 'whole' leads to popular misconceptions in stories involving the increase and decrease of an amount by the same fraction. For example, prices may go up by 10% and then go down by 10%. Enrolment for a certain club may increase by 1/5 in a year and then decrease by 1/5 the year after. The intuitive expectation in these cases is that these changes cancel each other out resulting in the initial amount. However, this is obviously not the case since the relative increase and the decrease are referring to different amounts. That is, the fraction or the percentage is taken from a different 'whole'. The misconception is well documented in the research literature. Our hope, maybe a naïve one, is that the story of bears and apples may draw students' explicit attention to the consideration of the 'reference whole' whenever the successful solution of a problem depends on such a consideration.

CHAPTER 9

STORIES THAT TELL A JOKE

Mathematics is made of 50 percent formulas, 50 percent proofs, and 50 percent imagination. (Anonymous)

The Talmud says, "Start every lesson with a humorous illustration" (Pesachim, 117a). This is no less true for a lesson on mathematics. In Chapter 2 we mentioned humour as a desired component of a story, a component that can enhance both the telling and the hearing of a story. We have also exemplified how humour can be inserted, either as a situation that invites a smile or the choice of attributes or descriptors that are involved. It is likely that in previous chapters the reader has identified a variety of humorous undertones in our stories, regardless of whether or not we have explicitly pointed to them. For example, in choosing one's outfit, we mentioned 37 hats. The impossibility of this raises a smile, but also helps in understanding mathematical ideas we wish students to acquire. We also mentioned earlier that Archimedes' colleague Bartholomew retired to Jamaica and is making circles for the tourists. And, of course, there are countless opportunities to insert humour in stories that have not been mentioned. For example, what was farmer Jake doing as he waited for the crow to return to the barn? Maybe, he was just sitting there, dying of boredom. But maybe he surfed the internet to find information on how to get rid of a crow, or just to download rap music. We trust that the teacher, the story teller, will choose the appropriate activity of farmer Jake, which could be close to students' current interests and appear unrelated to the "once upon a time" world of farmers. We believe that inserting pieces of information that may have little relevance to the mathematical ideas in the story contributes to creating humorous situations and ultimately helps in keeping students engaged as active listeners.

In this section we focus on a special kind of a short story – a joke – that is only rarely mentioned in education and is almost always ignored in mathematics education. We consider how carefully chosen jokes can contribute to classroom practice. Of course any kind of a joke, if appropriately selected and used, can contribute to a supportive atmosphere and good feelings, and as such, indirectly influence learning. But we discuss here a special kind of joke – a joke related to mathematics: mathematics learning, understanding, mathematical language and informal assessment.

CHAPTER 9

WARMING UP

There are three kinds of mathematicians: those who can count and those who can't.

Of course this joke has a greater effect if told by a mathematician, one of those who can't count. The humour in this case is a result of creating an expectation and then breaking it. Putting this differently, a necessary ingredient of humour is that two incongruous ways of viewing something (a person, a sentence or a situation) are juxtaposed.

Here are a few less-sophisticated examples, situated in the context of arithmetic.

Teacher: Name six animals of the Arctic region
Student: Three walruses and three polar bears

Student: Which is correct– five plus four is eleven or five plus four are eleven?
Teacher: Neither. Five plus four is nine.

Fran: Dad, can you help me find the greatest common denominator?
Dad: Good heavens, girl! Haven't they found that yet? They have been looking for it since I was your age.

Teacher: If your father had ten dollars and you asked him for six dollars, how many dollars would your father have left?
Student: Ten
Teacher: You don't know your maths.
Student: You don't know my father.

Teacher: If you add 456 and 1098, what do you get?
Student: A wrong answer.

Question: Why did the math book commit suicide?
Answer: It had too many problems.

Egan (1997) notes that jokes can be used to make children reflect on the language they use and to create awareness of language. Similarly, mathematical jokes can point to the subtleties of mathematical language and to the subtleties of intention and the implicit underlying assumptions. Most efficient in this regard are jokes or riddles that require prior knowledge and acquaintance with a specific topic in order to fully appreciate them. Consider for example the following scenario:

Angry wife: You said you will be home by 11:45, now it is 3am!
Mathematically inclined husband: I said I will arrive at quarter of 12, I'm exactly on time, dear.

Of course one does not learn what is a *quarter of 12* from this joke. However, through this joke prior knowledge is highlighted and reinforced in a new way. Such prior knowledge is necessary in order to appreciate many mathematical jokes.

Q: What is purple and commutes to work?
A: An Abelian grape.

We believe that only a few readers find this funny. They are those that have the concept of commutativity and of a mathematical structure called a group in their immediate repertoire and recall that commutative groups are also referred to as Abelian groups, named after the renowned Norwegian mathematician Niels Henrik Abel. In an Abelian group all the elements 'commute', that is, satisfy the property of commutativity, a*b=b*a. This example also highlights another feature of humour – if a joke requires an explanation it does not present any humour to a hearer. Nevertheless we introduce this example to emphasize the importance of prior knowledge in perceiving humour. Cohen (1999) refers to such a joke as 'hermetic' – a background condition for which knowledge or belief is required. Most people refer to it as an 'inside' joke. A more elementary example is presented in the following teacher's announcement to the class:

The problems on the test will be similar to those we solved in class. Of course the numbers will be different. But not all of them. π will still be 3.14159...

We believe this may reinforce, not the specific value of π (pi), but the learner's appreciation of it as a constant. As such, a joke may serve a teacher as an informal assessment tool.

JOKES AND LANGUAGE

Why was 6 afraid of 7?
Because 7-8-9 (seven ate nine)

Twelve pairs hanging high,
Twelve knights riding by
Each knight took a pear,
And yet left a dozen there

These teasers each have mathematical content, such as the counting sequence or awareness that the number 12 indicates a dozen. However, the joke here is in the pun presented by homonyms, which makes it more effective when told and heard rather than when decoded from a written text. These jokes *use* mathematical content, but they are not *about* mathematics. They are language dependent, that is, the humour is lost when the joke is translated to another language. These could be

CHAPTER 9

valuable examples of humour for integrating mathematics and English or supporting ESL learners, who may need to stretch themselves to perceive subtlety.

Our next examples present a different kind of homonymy – words that have different meanings in mathematics and in natural language.

> *Teacher: What do we do to increase the volume?*
> *Student: Turn the knob!*

> *There were 3 guests at a tea party, and 20 sugar cubes in a sugar bowl. Each guest put an odd number of cubes in her tea. They used all 20 sugar cubes. What number of cubes could each guest use?*

While the first example is simply intended to invite a smile, the second example invites an activity. In fact, we often introduce the sugar cubes example as an invitation to explore and prove some of the properties of even and odd numbers. After several minutes of trial and error students usually come up with an argument that the sum of three odd numbers must be odd, and therefore the sum cannot be 20. We could wait several minutes as students try to convince one another that these conditions cannot be possible. Then we say:

> "*Actually, it was 1, 1 and 18.*"
> "*But 18 is not and odd number!*" – is an expected comment from students.
> "*But it is an odd number of sugar cubes to put into your tea, isn't it?*"

To overcome the feeling of being 'cheated', that some students experience after presenting a convincing mathematical argument for impossibility of the event, the teacher may present a truly mathematical solution, though a tricky one. Make one 'big' cube of sugar out of 8 small sugar cubes. The 3 possible odd numbers are 1 (big cube), 5 and 7. Of course having suggested this solution to students we expect a healthy argument about its validity and the intended interpretation of the problem.

Humorous situations can also be created around the intended meaning of mathematical statement and questions.

> *Teacher: How many times can you subtract 3 from 12?*
> *Student: As many as I want, but I always get 9.*

The teacher's question above is often used as a shortcut to represent division as repeated subtraction. A possible way to interpret the division of 12 by 3 is to imagine how many 3-unit pieces can be cut from a 12-unit piece. As discussed in Chapter 7 in relation to division by 0, this interpretation is known as the measurement or quotitive view of division, in contrast to the partitive view, where division is perceived as putting objects into equivalent sets. Recall that cutting shorter pieces from a longer piece invites the image of repeated subtraction:

12-3-3-3-3 = 0, therefore the answer to 12÷3 is 4.

However, this repeated subtraction is often referred to as "subtracting 3 from 12, 4 times" to get 0, where the intended meaning is that in each subtraction the minuend (the number we subtract from) is the result of the previous subtraction. The 'smarty pants' answer of the student above is an excellent way to point learners' attention to the possibility of a different interpretation of a conventional meaning.

JOKES ABOUT MATHEMATICIANS

A popular type of hermetic jokes that we wish to mention are jokes about mathematicians. Background understanding requires some familiarity with mathematicians' ways of thinking.

> *An engineer, a physicist, and a mathematician are shown a pasture with a herd of sheep, and told to put them inside the smallest possible length of a fence. The engineer is first. He herds the sheep into a circle and then puts the fence around them, declaring, "A circle will use the least fence for a given area, so this is the best solution." The physicist is next. She creates a circular fence of infinite radius around the sheep, and then draws the fence tight around the herd, declaring, "This will give the smallest circular fence around the herd." The mathematician is last. After giving the problem a little thought, he puts a small fence around himself and then declares, "I define myself to be on the outside and the sheep to be on the inside!"*

> *A chemist, a physicist, and a mathematician are stranded on an island when a can of food rolls ashore. The chemist and the physicist struggle to comes up with a way to open the can. Then suddenly the mathematician gets a bright idea: "Assume we have a can opener ..."*

Another nice story-joke that relates to mathematical ways of thinking is about a mathematician who boils water. The story goes something like this:

> *There is a kettle in the bedroom (and how it got there is another story), there is stove in the kitchen and there is a mathematician who wants to boil some water to make himself a cup of tea. So he (always he! at least in this story) takes the kettle from the bedroom brings it to the kitchen, boils the water and makes himself a cup of tea.*

Where is the joke? It's coming (maybe).

> *So now we have a new problem. The kettle is now in the kitchen and our mathematician wants to boil some water to make another cup of tea. What does he do? Well, he brings the kettle into the bedroom – and now he has a problem he has already solved.*

Our students are often stunned with this joke and their smiles often indicate their politeness rather than their understanding. But this story-joke represents the profound essence of mathematical experience: we derive new information based on known facts, we build new algorithms from known ones, we redress problems to

CHAPTER 9

make them look familiar. Such examples of building on past knowledge are countless: we (may) derive the formula for the area of a triangle by considering the known area of a rectangle; we (may) derive multiplication facts based on known addition facts; we base operations with integers on the previously known operations with whole numbers, etc.

Let us return for a moment to the famous Gaussian solution for the sum of 100 numbers (discussed earlier in Chapter 2). An extension of the pairing strategy provided us with a method for finding the sum of an even set of numbers. What if the set of numbers is odd? Several solutions are possible. We exemplify those by considering the sum of natural numbers up to 17:

- 'hide' the last number 17 and then add it to sum of an even number of addends, given by considering 8 pairs with the sum of 17 in each
    $8 \times 17 + 17 = 153$
- 'hide' the first number 1 and then add it to the sum of the even number of addends, given by considering 8 pairs with the sum of 19 in each
    $8 \times 19 + 1 = 153$
- 'ignore' the middle number 9 and then add it to the sum of the even number of addends, given by considering 8 pairs with the sum of 18 in each
    $8 \times 18 + 9 = 153$
- 'double' the sum by rearranging the numbers in reversed order next to the original sequence, which results in 17 pairs with the sum of 18 in each, and then take half of the result

1	2	3	4	5	6	7	8	9	10	11	12	13	14	15	16	17
17	16	15	14	13	12	11	10	9	8	7	6	5	4	3	2	1

$18 \times 17 \div 2 = 153$

Regardless of which strategy one chooses – and before algebra teachers fit everything into one formula – each strategy is supported by a 'known' solution presented in Gauss' pairing method. "Think of a similar but simpler problem" is a powerful heuristic discussed in detail by Polya in his classical book *How to Solve it* (Polya, 1945/1988). If nothing else, it can be introduced as a directive to follow, or it can be introduced with a story. Reference to the familiar is what assists mathematicians in solving problems, in proving theorems and, occasionally, in boiling water.

This is getting too mathematical in a chapter on humour and jokes. So let's turn to another joke that may reveal something about mathematical way of thinking:

A mathematician, a biologist and a physicist are sitting in a street café watching people going in and coming out of the house on the other side of the street. First they see two people going into the house. Time passes. After a while they notice three people coming out of the house.

The Physicist: "The measurement wasn't accurate."

The Biologists conclusion: "They have reproduced".

The Mathematician: "If now exactly 1 person enters the house then it will be empty again."

PRECISION WITH A SMILE

A joke can also emphasize one of the greatest virtues of mathematical thinking – precision and rigor.

A biologist, a statistician and a mathematician are on a photo-safari in Africa. They drive out on the savannah in their jeep, stop and scout the horizon with their binoculars.

The biologist: "Look! There's a herd of zebras! And there, in the middle: A white zebra! It's fantastic! There are white zebras! We'll be famous!"

The statistician: "It's not significant. We only know there's one white zebra.

The mathematician: "Actually, we know only that there exists one zebra, which is white on one side.

Precision is often required from students not only with respect to reasoning, but also with respect to measurement. But there is a catch. On one hand we wish for students to learn to measure precisely. On the other hand we also want them to understand that every measurement is an approximation, and the degree of required precision depends on a situation. In hoping to instil this understanding in students we could explain this idea several times, in many different ways – or, we could refer to a joke:

The guard in a museum was asked: "How old is the mummy?"

"5 thousand and 3 years, 4 months and 5 days" – he replied.

"And how would you know that for sure"

"The day I started to work here there was a sign that said the mummy was 5000 years old, and that was 3 years, 4 months and 5 days ago."

A joke like that can serve as a springboard for a discussion of measurement and appropriate choice of precision for any given purpose. In addition, jokes serve as an implicit assessment tool: students' smiles will reveal whether they 'got it' and give teacher an indication of the degree of their understanding of mathematical content, language or ideas.

SELF REFERENCE AND HUMOUR

A different and slightly more sophisticated source of mathematical humour is in self-reference. We bring it here for reader's smile, rather than specific curricular connection.

CHAPTER 9

A kitchen sign says:
House rules
   (#1) Mom is always right
   (#2) If mom is wrong, consult rule #1

Hofstadter's Law:
It always takes longer than you expect, even when you take into account Hofstadter's Law. (Hofstadter, 1980, p. 152)

SUMMARY

We summarize this section with a smile. We do not expect to be able to find or invent a joke appropriate for any mathematical topic. Similarly, we do not suggest that any story can or should be enhanced with humour. However, when this is possible, we believe, a positive learning outcome is to be expected.

Humorous mathematical short stories are also found in brain teasers, trick questions, or riddles. Such conundrums are often more intellectual than jokes while at the same time less rigorous than mathematics. As such these stories may act as a bridge between humour and mathematics. Furthermore, these conundrums possess one of the main characteristics of humour – the disjunction between what is anticipated and what is eventually revealed. That is, the answers to these questions or riddles are often unexpectedly simple and, once revealed, obvious. As such, they mimic the effect of a 'punch line'.

"Both mathematics and humour are forms of intellectual play, the emphasis in mathematics being more on the intellectual, in humour more on the play" (Paulos, 1980, p. 10). Bringing these together in a story serves to create levity in the context of an intellectual activity that is often perceived as being devoid of humour. So, if you wish to follow the Talmud's suggestion and start every lesson with a humorous illustration – there are ample opportunities to be found. However, our practice is directed towards *enriching* every lesson with a humorous illustration, rather than *starting* with it.

CHAPTER 10

CREATING A STORY

In previous chapters we introduced or recaptured several stories. We also considered components that make stories engaging for learners, such as conflict, imagery, wonder, and humour. However, where do stories come from? If a teacher believes that a story is a creative and appropriate way to engage students with mathematics, how is a good story found? ... chosen? ... created? In this chapter we demonstrate how instruction of specific mathematical topics or concepts can be planned and implemented, that is, we provide what we refer to as a 'planning framework'. In what follows we first present the framework, explain its various components and then exemplify the planning of instructional and learning activities according to this framework. We purposefully avoid the terms 'lesson planning' or 'unit planning'. For our purposes, an instructional and learning activity can be a part of a lesson, an entire lesson, or can even be extended over a series of lessons.

PLANNING FRAMEWORK

Out framework includes the following components, on which we elaborate below.
– Identifying the target.
– Identifying the problem (mathematical problem or problematic issue).
– Identifying the story. Exploring what tools are appropriate to support the plot and present the problem in a way that engages students.
– Organizing the presentation of the problem using story telling. Considering students' possible engagement.
– Extending or varying the initial problem situation (optional).
– Conclusion, closure.

Identifying the target

Identification of a target is essential before the actual planning can begin. A target may take many different forms. It can be a fragment of curriculum content, such as a specific concept or topic. It can be related to a specific formula, method or strategy. It can also be a meta-content, such as applicability or beauty of some mathematical idea or method. Furthermore, our target can be what is identified in different curriculum documents as a 'standard' or 'intended learning outcome'. And of course it can be any combination of these.

For example, in the story of *The King's Will* (see Chapter 7) the specific concept targeted is division by zero. In the story of *The Pirates and the Buried Treasure* (see Chapter 6) the targeted concept is that of a standard unit of measurement and

CHAPTER 10

the meta-content relates to its usefulness and applicability. In the story of *Gauss and His Teacher* (see Chapter 2) the curriculum content we are targeting is related to the topic of patterns in elementary school, or the sum of the elements of an arithmetic sequence in secondary school; the specific strategy is the pairing summation method and the meta-content is the internal simplicity and power of this method. In the story of *Grains on a Chessboard* (see Chapter 6) the target is the appreciation of exponential growth.

Identifying the problem

Once the curriculum content is identified, the questions to be addressed are: What is the mathematical problem or activity that can engage the learner with the given content? Is there anything problematic about the specific target? How can the problem or the problematic be presented in the form of a story? It is through the examination of these questions that we can begin to explore resources and examine possibilities.

The most easily accessible, and at times the only, resource is personal knowledge. Experienced teachers know where learners have difficulties and know how to get past these difficulties. Where immediate personal knowledge does not serve the needs, we turn to books, children's stories, colleagues, or the internet in order to find mathematical problems or snapshots of existing mathematical folklore and historical anecdotes.

Identifying the story and supporting tools

The story itself can be dry and uninviting when presented without an emotional context. However, these 'barebones; versions can eventually become an engaging story or activity. Consider for example the following plot – "Cinderella lost her shoe and the prince found her based on this shoe". The details are correct, but the emotions are lost.

Similarly, in relation to our mathematical theme, consider the task – "find the sum of the numbers from 1 to 100". For the majority of students this would not capture their interest. In teaching we are not interested in these 'barebones' versions. Our task is to present a problem in a way that is engaging, memorable and which captures a student's imagination. This is where we turn to stories and the repertoire of cognitive tools that were introduced, discussed and exemplified in previous chapters and take advantage of their ability to engage the imagination.

Of course there is no expectation that all these tools will appear in every problem or every lesson. We consider them as a menu to choose from, acknowledging that we will always attempt to chose several menu items and that some items will appear more frequently than others in our choices.

Almost every mathematical problem can be presented using some story plot. At times our exploration will not be extremely fruitful and we will feel blessed if able to find or create one scenario for a story. At other times we will be faced with a variety of possible plots and be forced to make a choice. The needs of our students and the awareness of what can best grab their attention in this day and age will help as guiding factors in choosing a plot.

Where we are *locating wonder* depends not only on the target itself, but also on the chosen problem. For example, in targeting the area of a circle we can locate wonder around the regularity of some relations of measures, around efficiency and accuracy of some calculations, or around the personas of mathematicians who explored this topic.

Exposure of a conflict may create a deeper imaginative engagement. A dark drawing is seen more clearly when presented on a bright background. A method is seen as more powerful when brought in contrast with a weak one. A counsellor is seen as more clever if accompanied by a clueless one. Furthermore, descriptive *images* can enhance any story by adding details that make stories more memorable and more interesting to listen to. Some can be presented from a *humorous* angle, while others can focus on the *human* relevance, capitalizing on applicability or the power of invention.

A careful examination of the target itself may guide our choice of the cognitive tools. We ask, what is the mathematical relevance or applicability of the target? What if it didn't exist? What if it were different? These 'what if' questions serve as a wonderful tool in creating narrative for problem situations and locating wonder around them.

For example, suppose we teach division in grades 3 or 4 and we want to emphasize not just the algorithm but the meaning of this operation in relation to other mathematical operations. Historical resources may tell us that up until the 17th century division was taught only in prestigious universities. This could make a nice story to tell, but, unfortunately, this historical anecdote will be of no use in helping students understand possible meanings of the division operation. Therefore we turn to the resource of asking "What if not? What if there was no division operation available to you, how would you be able to share 528 marbles among 6 friends?" A narrative can address a 'forbidden' operation or simply a broken calculator key and a need to perform many division operations rather quickly. Will the calculator still be of any help? Will there be an opportunity to verify answers? These questions will leave our students wondering. In the resulting activity students will be guided to reinvent the long division algorithm, to reinforce the connection between division and multiplication, and – what is often ignored in the curriculum – to explore the connection between division and repeated subtraction.

Organizing the presentation of the problem

We believe that the power of a problem, and its potential contribution to a learner, depends on how its related story is presented. If our problem is embedded in a story, how the story is told is crucial. We always attempt to tell a story in an interactive fashion, even if the story is read from a book.

There are several ways to create interaction with students around the problem. One possibility is to pause and have students complete a sentence or make a suggestion. This 'attention grabbing' interaction has been exemplified in the story

CHAPTER 10

of *A Crow and a Farmer* (Chapter 3). Such interaction can be further extended by having students tell parts of the story. This is especially powerful if a story has a repeating pattern in it. Interaction through a story can also be mathematical in nature. Students can be asked to answer simple questions or engage in exploration or an activity. In previous chapters we acknowledged a variety of mathematical problems and activities that are introduced by stories or weave through stories. Consider, for example, counting the teachers' outfits, calculating the number of rice grains on a chessboard, or drawing and measuring polygons inside circles.

As mentioned earlier, humorous overtones contribute greatly to the presentation of a problem. If the situation itself lacks humour then humour can be introduced through a choice of names, numbers, or setting.

Beyond the problem (Extending or varying the initial problem situation)

Presentation of the material through an engaging story is only one step towards accomplishing curricular objectives. There is also a place for problem solving, exploration activities, and even drill and practice to reach and master curriculum content. However, we believe that material introduced through the capitalization on stories creates a favourable atmosphere for learning and makes the activities of problem solving, exploration, and drill and practice more appealing. As mentioned earlier, the intention of some stories is only to introduce a topic or concept, while the intention of other stories is to weave itself through a topic. In this latter situation, and in the best case scenario, the follow up activities will be related to the story. For example, in exploring the sums of different sequences (not just numbers from 1 to 100) we can always consider "how would Gauss or his classmates have done it"?

Closure

One possible way to conclude a lesson or a topic is to connect the activity back to the initial problem situation. We tried to exemplify this on several occasions in the preceding chapter. In the story of *Grains on the Chessboard* (Chapter 6) students encounter a story, engage in a calculation, are faced with the enormity of the result, and only then does the story continue with "what actually happened". Similarly, in the story of *The Pirates and the Buried Treasure* (Chapter 6), students encounter the story, discuss possibilities, make and test conjectures, and only then is the story brought to its conclusion.

In a different concluding exercise we could invite the students to write the conclusion or extension of the story, to introduce a different but related problem, or to write the next chapter. What happened in Gauss' class the next day? What did Archimedes do after his bath? What if the absent-minded mathematician had to boil milk and not water? The history books do not tell us. Maybe the students will.

In what follows we exemplify how this framework can be used to plan for instruction through the use of two elaborated examples and one abbreviated example. We further suggest how these examples can be adapted or extended for different populations of students.

EXAMPLE OF PLANNING 1 (ELABORATED): AREA AND PERIMETER

For this example we are going to explore how the framework could be brought to bear on the topic of the area and perimeter of a rectangle in general and the relationship between these two measures in particular. We chose this topic in part because of the wealth of resources associated with it. This may seem to make our task of identifying a problem and creating an imaginatively engaging lesson rather easy, but this is not at all the case. The richness of resources, which are largely manipulative based, makes choosing a good problem to follow more difficult. The other reason we chose this particular example is because this topic is often categorized as one where there is very little 'stuff' to teach. After all, for a rectangle, perimeter is just the sum of the sides and area is easily found by multiplying the length by the width. However, it is just such thinking that contributes to the widespread mistreatment of the topic that often results in an impoverished, if not completely absent, understanding of the concepts of area and perimeter.

For this particular example we present the development of the lesson as it adheres to the framework introduced in the previous section.

Identifying the target: Area and Perimeter of a rectangle

As already mentioned, our target is the area and the perimeter of a rectangle, with a focus on the relationship between the two. This is a specific curriculum item, the teaching of which would typically span several lessons and would cover, among other things the formulas for the area and perimeter of a rectangle. The separate consideration of area and perimeter and an understanding of these measures is a prerequisite for exploring the relationship between the two.

For example, the NCTM Standards (2000, p.170) identify the following as being relevant to the concept of area and perimeter of rectangular regions:
– Understand such attributes as length, area, weight, volume, and size of angle and select appropriate type of unit for measuring each attribute.
– Explore what happens to measurement of a two-dimensional shape such as its perimeter and area when the shape is changed in some way.
– Develop, understand, and use formulas to find the area of rectangles and related triangles and parallelograms.

Identifying the problem

The problematic issue that we are going to attend to is the relationship between perimeter and area of a rectangle.
    Consider the following pairs of rectangles:
        (a) 3 by 4 and 2 by 6

(b) 1 by 7 and 2 by 6
(c) 2 by 11 and 4 by 6

In each pair, identify which is smaller and which is larger, or whether they are the same size.

In the wording of the problem, we specifically avoid mentioning the criterion by which the rectangles are to be compared. And herein lies the problem: in (a) the rectangles are equal in area, but not in perimeter; in (b) the rectangles are equal in perimeter, but not in area; and in (c), which is the most surprising case, a rectangle which is larger in perimeter, is smaller in area. Research shows that these cases are problematic for students because there is a tendency to assume that being larger in one attribute implies being larger in another. This has been identified as "the more of A, the more of B" intuitive rule and instances of the application of such a rule are described in detail by Stavy and Tirosh (2000).

What appeals to us here is the fact that this is not such an absurd conclusion to arrive at. Our daily experiences constantly reinforce the fact that if a rectangle is bigger in its perimeter, it is also bigger in its area. In fact, it is only the extreme cases where the rectangles are long and skinny that this relationship does not hold. It is definitely possible to direct students' attention to the relationship by a 'barebones' presentation of a problem such as above, provoking disagreement among students and fruitful discussion. However, for us, such discordance between common sense intuition and mathematical fact offers a rich and fertile ground for an engaging and memorable story.

Identifying the story

We now are about to create a story. However, a variety of problems related to area and perimeter can be created and embedded in stories. Which ones could be most engaging for students?

With regards to mathematical relevance, the calculation of the area and the perimeter of a rectangle has countless uses, from figuring out how much paint is required to paint a bedroom, doghouse, or tree fort to calculating how much wrapping paper is required to wrap a birthday present. Such richness in applicability can be found in many elementary mathematics topics and it is often presented in textbooks and teacher resource guides as part of suggested instructional strategies. However, this is also a bit of a 'red herring'. Various choices of 'real life' applicability all have one thing in common: the students do not care about them. Although these examples are all snapshots of reality, they are not our students' reality. Having said that, however, this richness of applicability means that the need to calculate the area and/or the perimeter can be built into almost any storyline.

We chose to focus on a specific anecdote from ancient Egypt that integrates historical background with a human aspect of mathematical engagement. Every year in Egypt the Nile would rise and flood all the farmland wiping out the individual farm boundaries. In the spring after the Nile had receded all these boundaries would have to be re-established through surveying and the use of geometry. This is where geometry gets its name – geometry means to measure (metry) the land (geo).

The historical anecdote about Egypt shows great promise as the basis for an engaging story. Even in its much abbreviated telling it already had many of the elements discussed in the earlier parts of this book. The applicability of the mathematics offers a variety of directions in which to create a story. We explore the possible plot lines in the context of the cognitive tools examined in the previous chapters. The first of these is to locate wonder. Egypt presents a source rich in wonder; from the annual rising of the Nile to the splendour of this ancient civilization there is much to be in awe of. However, we will also place wonder in the mathematics we have chosen to explore. Our goal is to get students to wonder about the relationship between the perimeter and area of a rectangle; to see that it is indeed possible to vary the area while keeping the perimeter fixed. To accomplish this we create a situation in which perimeter is used incorrectly as a measure of size of a rectangular region. Further moulding is possible with the help of a conflict.

To create a conflict in and around the measure of farmland there are again several options available to us. We could create a situation where land is being traded, or bought and sold, and the unit of measure of land size is its perimeter. There could be a shrewd businessman who knows how to buy farmlands in such a system that produces the largest amount of crops. Pitted against this shrewd businessman could be a second character that every year seems to pay the same, but get much less for his money. So, he decides to figure out how this businessman manages to do this, and so on. Another conflict that we could construct is between a man and his evil brother who have to divide up a piece of land that their father has left them, or three brothers having to do the same. There are lots of opportunities to create conflicts within such stories. However, we have chosen to create a character that the students can better identify with, a boy their age. This boy, and we will find a suitable name for him, is pitted against the tax collector who collects tax based on farm size. We set the story so that the measure of land is its perimeter, and the boy sees an injustice in this that he strives (against overwhelming odds) to right. We further accentuate the story with images, humour and detail to enhance the telling, and the hearing, of the story.

Presentation of the problem, telling of a story

> 5000 years ago in the land that is now called Egypt there was a small farming community named Menutis. Every year the mighty Nile would swell and overflow its banks, flooding the farms of Menutis. As the waters receded they left behind the silt of the river, nourishing the soil, and making Menutis the best place in Egypt to grow melons. Menutis was well known for its melons. They were the sweetest in the land, and over the years many farmers had come from all over Egypt to make Menutis their home. One such farmer was Kashta, who had come to Menutis when he was a young man, bought a small farm, and had worked the land with skill and caring

CHAPTER 10

for so many years. Kashta loved his farm. He loved to watch the sunrise from his field as it heralded a new day. He loved to watch the sunset from the bank of the Nile, which bordered his farm on one side. As the sun sank below the horizon the sound of the crickets would erupt from the reeds that grew along the shore and sing to him the sweetest of melodies. But more than anything he loved his young son, Besenmut who worked with him in the field, and walked with him along the bank of the Nile in the evening when the day was done.

Years passed and Kashta was no longer a young man, he was getting quite old, and he knew that the day would come soon that his son would have to take over the farm. This used to trouble Kashta greatly. For, you see, Besenmut was only 9 years old, and small for his age. Kashta used to worry how this small boy would ever manage to run a farm. But, even though Besenmut was only 9 years old, and even though he was small, he was smart. Kashta knew in his heart that the boy would find a way to manage things. And so it was, one day Kashta was too old to work the farm anymore and Besenmut took over.

Well, it didn't take long before Besenmut got the hang of things, and that year he brought to the market melons that were just as sweet, and just as big, as the ones his father had grown. Kashta was very proud of his young son, and as they shared their evening walk along the bank of the Nile he used to tell him so. He would say that the crickets sang for Besenmut now, for he was the best farmer in Menutis.

One day, not long after Besenmut had sold his harvest at the market, the tax collector came to their house to collect the annual property tax. The tax collector was a strange little man who talked to himself as he walked. He was short, and round, and very unkempt, with bits of food spilled on his clothes, and the strangest habit of sneezing every time he said the word 'no'. Actually, he didn't even have to say the word, he just had to think it and he would sneeze. This used to amuse Besenmut a great deal. Well, it did when he was eight years old and didn't understand what this 'tax' business was all about. He would ask the tax collector question upon question to which he knew the answer would be 'no', just to see this little round man sneeze himself into a tizzy. But this year Besenmut wasn't amused. This year Besenmut wasn't amused at all. This year Besenmut was told he had to give some of the money he had earned to this strange little man. Besenmut had never heard of such a thing. After all, let's get real here, he was only 9 years old. So Besenmut asked his father and the tax collector what this was all about. "Well," – Kashta began, – "every year all the farmers in Menutis have to pay tribute to our ruler. We do this by giving a portion of our earnings to the tax collector."

Besenmut didn't understand this, he wanted to understand, but he didn't. He had so many questions. But the tax collector was already impatient with

> this young boy who had always tormented him so. He snapped at Besenmut, "See here young boy, as the farmer of this land you are obligated to pay tax on it."
>
> "And how much tax am I to pay?" Besenmut snapped back.
>
> "32 copper coins, two for each tygep around your farm." I should point out at this point that a tygep was a way of measuring distance in ancient Egypt. One tygep is about as long as a school bus. I should also tell you that the farm that Besinmut and his father lived on was a rectangle that was 6 tygeps along one edge and 2 tygeps along the other.
>
> "This is fair, Besenmut," said Kashta to his young son, "This is what I have paid every year. This is what our neighbour to the south has paid every year, and this is what our neighbour to the north has paid every year. We all pay the same. See, it's fair."
>
> It was true that each of their neighbours had a farm that was 16 tygeps around; the farm to the south was 7 tygeps by 1 tygep, and the farm to the north was 4 tygeps by 4 tygeps. But Besenmut wasn't sure that this way of paying the taxes was fair. After all, this year the farmer to the south brought a very small amount of melons to the market, much less than Besenmut did. At the same time, the farmer to the north brought many more melons to the market than Besenmut did. So Besenmut protested. "This means of taxation that you use is not fair. We all pay the same, but we don't produce the same."
>
> The tax collector replied, "This is how we do it. This is how we have always done it. If you don't like it you may speak at the tribunal about it. In seven days time they are meeting to discuss the taxation plan."

At this point in the story we pause the narration and ask the students a series of questions. Was Besenmut correct? Was the system unfair? Could you find a way to show that it was unfair? We would allow the students lots of time to think about these questions. The purpose is to get them to discuss, conjecture, and propose solutions. Perhaps they would write about it in journals, or work in groups. They could discuss whether the amount of melons produced represents correctly the size of the farms. As the students' discussion evolves, the narrator may provide further detail.

> Besenmut was certain that this system was unfair. After all, as good a farmer as his father (and now himself) was, their neighbour to the north was no better. Likewise, their farmer to the south was no worse. They weren't all producing different amounts of melons based on farming ability. Further, the land was fertile in all the farms. Besenmut felt that somehow their farms were different sizes. He needed a way to show this. The tribunal would never listen to him if he couldn't find a convincing and simple way to show that the farms were different sizes. The method of measuring around the outside of the farm had been used for all these years, since before his

CHAPTER 10

father's father's time, he was told, because it was easy, and everybody knew how to do it. Besenmut needed to show it was wrong, and he needed to find a fair, yet easy, way to measure the size of the farms.

How could he show that the current way of measuring the farmland size was wrong? What would be a better method of measuring the size of the farm?

Beyond the story (Extending or varying the initial problem situation)

We stop the story here. It is now up to the teacher to provide the time and the support to the students to allow them to discover a solution. A really effective way to show that the farms are different sizes is to cut out scale models of them using paper. The 1x7 can then be shown to fit almost into the 2x6. The piece that sticks out can be cut off and used as the unit of measure. Once this is established, the areas of all the farms can be determined using the same measuring unit. From considering more examples of local farms the formula can emerge.

The story can also be continued by exploring an extension in which Besenmut must not only convince the tribunal that area is a better measure of a farm's size, but also figure out a new taxation system based on this fact – a taxation system that sees the same amount of money coming into the king's coffers.

Alternatively, the story can be changed to a case where the area is fixed and the perimeter is changed. This will examine the same relationship between area and perimeter with the added benefit of presenting, perhaps for the first time, the idea of thought experiment and extreme cases. For as a rectangle is stretched longer and longer, and the width is simultaneously allowed to get smaller and smaller, it is possible to maintain a fixed area. Consider for example all the possible rectangles with the area of 48 square units. As an additional route for mathematical exploration, restricting the dimensions of a rectangular area to whole numbers allows us to segue into multiple factorizations of whole numbers and the idea of primes.

Closure

There are several ways to conclude this mathematical activity. We can return to the narration of the story, telling how Besenmut approached the tribunal and how his ideas were received. But in the case of Besenmut we recommend allowing the students to complete the story. The stage is well set for this.

Upon conclusion it would be prudent on the part of the teacher to clarify some of the creative liberties that were taken with this story. Although the names that were used were authentic, and melons were indeed grown in ancient Egypt, there is no such thing as a tygep for a unit of measure. We invented it to keep the dimensions small, while at the same time giving the students a tangible and imaginable measurement standard.

CREATING A STORY

EXAMPLE OF PLANNING 2 (LESS ELABORATED): TELLING TIME

Identifying the target and the problem: Reading an analogue clock

Numerous reports from teachers indicate that many students experience difficulty in learning to determine time with an analogue clock. This may be due to curriculum approaches that often teach children to first read clocks to the hour, then the half hour, and finally quarter hours. As a result, a child who can successfully determine what time the clock shows at 5:30, may be at loss at 5:38. Furthermore, starting instruction with two-handed clocks contributes to students' confusion between the hands and doesn't emphasize sufficiently the different functions of the two hands. Therefore we suggest starting with an hour-hand only.

Identifying the story and organizing the presentation of a problem

Once again, we choose a story and consider how its plot can be enriched. The 'barebones' version of the plot can be seen as follows: the chief of a tribe creates a one-handed clock to indicate the time of tribal gatherings; another hand is added later as a necessity for greater precision. We create images and emphasize human need as we bring the story to the students.

> *The chief of the Zalla tribe wished for all the heads of tribe families to come to his tent for consultation every afternoon. All the important decisions about tribal life were made at this consultation. So, every day, when the Chief had finished his afternoon nap a flag would be raised in front of his tent as an indicator that it was time for the Zalla gathering. But the tribe grew and different Zalla families erected their tents some distance from the main village, so they couldn't see the flag. How would they know that it was the time for gathering?*

[interaction]

> *The Chief tried drumming as a signal for the get-together, but it disturbed his wife and his grandchildren, who liked to take longer naps. So, after thinking about the problem for a long, long, long time, the chief invented a time-telling device, something like what we would call a clock. It was round and had the numbers 1 to 12 spread around its edge at equal distances. It had one hand that moved around the numbers at a constant speed, and completed exactly two rounds from one sunrise to the next. The chief named this clock an 'our' clock, because it told the people when 'our' meeting was. The Zalla chief made one of these devices for each family, and the family heads were told to come for a daily gathering exactly when the hand pointed to number 5. Do you think this would work?*

[interaction, activity]

> *In fact, it worked well for families who lived close to the chief's tent. They waited for the time-hand to point to 5, then they walked very quickly to the*

CHAPTER 10

Chief's tent and the time hand was still pointing at 5 when they arrived. However, for families who lived at a distance the task wasn't that easy. They left when the time-hand was pointing to 5, but when they arrived the time hand was pointing somewhere between 5 and 6. This made the Chief very mad. So the next time those who lived far away left their tents when the time hand was pointing to 4, and arrived when the time hand was somewhere between 4 and 5. This interrupted the Chief's nap and made him even angrier. Was there a solution? What would you suggest?

[activity]

Before we get to conclusion of this story let me tell you about something else that happened in this village. Every few years an eclipse would happen in the village. Do you know what an eclipse is? An eclipse is when the moon passes in front of the sun making it dark as night for a few minutes. Well, legend has it that if you live near the equator, as the Zalla did, you can balance an egg on its end on the day of an eclipse. Well, it's no legend. It is true, and the Zalla loved to do this. They loved it so much that they used to have contests to see who could balance an egg the longest. At first this was a simple matter of having a contest where everybody would line up and let go of their egg at the same time. But as the tribe got bigger and bigger it got more and more difficult to get everybody together to do this. This made the villagers very sad. The chief of the Zalla didn't like his tribe being sad. So, he thought, and he thought, and he thought. He thought for a whole year. And then he came up with a solution. He had invented a clock for getting the heads of families to meet at the right time, and although it didn't yet work that well, he thought that maybe he could do the same thing for the egg balancing contest. But the clock that he had already invented moved too slow. The best egg balancers could only hold their eggs balance for about as long as it took to walk around the village. This didn't allow the clock hand to get more than halfway between two of the clock numbers. He needed a clock that moved faster. So, he made a clock that didn't have any numbers on it. Instead it had 60 evenly spaced little marks around the outside of the circle and the hand, which was very long so that it almost reached the edge of the clock, would go once around in the time it took for the little hand on the 'our' clock to go between two numbers. The chief named this clock Minit's clock. Minit was the name of the Zalla warrior who had won the last egg balancing contest. This was a great idea. The villagers loved it. Now they were able to time how long an egg balanced for by counting how many little lines the hand passed as the egg balanced. They were even able to record how long the best balancers were able to balance their eggs for. The record was 34 Minit's clock marks.

Now, getting back to our story about the heads of families meeting with the chief when the hand of his clock points at 5. One day, the family head that lived furthest from the chief decided he was tired of always being late, or early, for the meeting. So, he decided he was going to find out exactly how long it took to get from his house to the chief's house. How do you think he did it?

[activity]

Indeed, he used the Minit's clock to time his walk. It turned out that it took 40 marks to get from his house to the chief's house. How did this help him get to the chief's house on time the next day?

[activity]

The next day, when he arrived right when the little hand on the 'our' clock was pointing at 5 the chief was very pleased. He asked how this had come to be. The man told him, and he told all the other family heads. And the next day, everyone was on time. This gave the chief a great idea. What do you think it was?

[closing activity and move to standard clock lesson]

By now the reader has easily recognized some elements in the story that contribute to students' imaginative engagement. These can, of course, be extended and reshaped as the storyteller desires.

In presenting the skeleton for this story we indicated possible places for interaction and inviting ideas from students. In addition, there is a need to integrate a variety of practice activities to connect the visual image of the clock hand to the time it is indicating. Furthermore, there is a need to introduce the language, that is, a short hand pointing exactly to 5 means "five o'clock". We recommend avoiding precision in the beginning, working with one clock hand only, students will indicate "this is a bit after 5" or "this is between 6 and 7 o'clock". Then they will strive for greater precision: "this is about half an hour past 5", "this is about quarter an hour before 6". The invention of the minutes hand is introduced as a solution for a need for precision.

There is also room in the story for a variety of problem-solving activities. For example, it takes Apachi 17 minutes to walk from his tent to the chief's. What time (tell and show) should he leave to arrive exactly at 5? Or, one day Apachi decided to take a long scenic stroll from the Zalla gathering back home. He left at 6:13 and arrived home at 7:05. How long did he walk? Of course an appropriate choice of numbers will adjust and gradually increase the level of difficulty.

Beyond the story and closure

Our story is open-ended and it invites a variety of extensions to reinforce the concept of analogue clock and time telling and also to expand on it. Students can make schedules for the tribal families and also organize their own schedules around the clock. Maybe the chief will announce a "perfect soft-boiled egg" contest, in which a precision to a minute is needed. Maybe there will be a running or arrow sharpening competition, which will introduce the need for a third

CHAPTER 10

(seconds) hand on a clock. In any case, almost any and all curriculum content related to telling time can be tied back to the original story.

EXAMPLE OF PLANNING 3 (ABBREVIATED): NUMBER PROPERTIES

Identifying the target

Three properties of numbers are approached in elementary school: commutative, associative and distributive. Commutative and associative properties hold for addition and multiplication, while the distributive property connects the two operations. A short algebraic description of these properties is as follows:

Commutative	a+b = b+a	a×b = b×a
Associative	(a+b)+c = a+(b+c)	(a×b)×c = a×(b×c)
Distributive	a×(b+c) = a×b + a×c	

Although algebraic expressions are often absent from elementary school curriculum, these rules are present in the curriculum in their numerical exemplification.

Identifying the problem and the problematic

The properties, when presented as such, are often devoid of any meaning. The existence of these properties is taken for granted by many students and the usage is limited. A 'barebones' presentation often results in "when are we ever gonna use this" reaction. Our goal is to have students experience the usefulness of the number properties. Rather than presenting or exemplifying the properties by the teacher we create a situation in which associativity and distributivity could be invented by the students. The problem situation we chose is as follows: Suppose one of the digit keys on the calculator is broken, but the rest work just fine. How is the ability to perform calculations affected?

Identifying the story, presenting the problem

Our story here is short, but it is chosen to locate students' wonder around the imaginary situation. Imagine that a calculator keys is broken ... say it is the 7 key. Does it mean that there are some calculations that cannot be carried out? Obviously, one cannot input a number like 74. But is there a way to perform a calculation involving this number?

The specific examples can be chosen to vary the difficulty to better fit the students' age and ability level. One possible starting point is to consider the sum 145+74 = ? Can you find the sum with the calculator? And even if it is easy and you already calculated the result mentally, can you verify this result with the broken key calculator?

One possible way is to approach this avoiding the 7-key is to enter 145+64+10. We suggest encouraging many possible ways and discussing variety. Examples may include 145+84-10, 145+44+30 etc.

After several examples a general property could be introduced: In fact, substituting 64+10 in place of 74, the sum 145+74 can be written as 145 + (64 + 10). This is the initial calculation. The sequence entered on the calculator performs (145+64) +10. So the calculator approach 'works' because the two expressions are equal: 145 + (64 + 10) = (145+64) +10

The fact that these two expressions are equal is a special property of numbers, with a long and funny name. It is up to the teacher whether and when the name – associativity or associative property – is introduced.

Of course there is often an option to choose paper and pencil calculations, but for students choosing this option we will present problems in which such calculations are lengthy and uninviting. Would you rather calculate 986,345 +777,777 or 567,765 + 78787 with paper and pencil or invent a calculator based approach avoiding the 7 key? If the paper and pencil approach is still preferred, we ask the labourers to verify their solution with the broken key calculator.

Extending or varying the initial problem situation

The simplest variation is to have the 7 key 'fixed', but now another key is broken. This will result in additional drill and practice. A more challenging situation may introduce more than one broken number key.

A different and probably more interesting extension may approach multiplication. How about 45×27? We found a way to deal with calculating addition using the calculator with the broken 7-key, but what about multiplication? A possible approach is to enter 45×9×3, which creates an opportunity for introducing the associative property for multiplication, exemplified in this case as 45×(9×3) = (45×9)×3.

And what about 145×74? Previously used strategy suggests representing 74 as 37×2 and entering the calculation of 145×37×2 . But this does not help if the 7-key on our calculator is still broken. Another set of possible calculations could involve 145×64 + 145×10 or 145×69 + 145×5. Exercises like this create the basis for introducing the distributive property, exemplified here as
145×(64+10) = (145×64) + (145×10).

Closure

We may invite students to write calculation exercises themselves and explore with a partner various ways of carrying and verifying the results with the broken key calculator. We also invite students to wonder and explore, is there a calculation that the broken key calculator will not be able to verify or to find a different way of performing? How about 77×77? To take advantage of the calculator in this case composition of number properties is required.

CHAPTER 11

STORIES OF A TEACHER AND HIS STUDENTS

We hope that by now we have convinced the reader of the value of stories in the mathematics classroom. But how does this really work? This chapter is an existence proof: we describe here several episodes from the classroom of a Vancouver teacher Mr. Chandra Balakrishnan, where he used the framework presented in Chapter 10 to create stories and story-based activities for his Grade 8 students and engaged students in writing stories and other creative literary endeavours (Balakrishnan, 2008). We describe some of this teacher's engagements using several of the same kinds of stories we introduced earlier: stories that introduce a concept, stories that accompany, stories that ask a question, and stories that introduce an activity.

EPISODE 1: STORY TO INTRODUCE A CONCEPT

The ideas of exponential growth are fascinating for learners. The speedy growth or decay is hard to grasp, especially when encountered for the first time. In Chapter 6 we mentioned the story of *The King's Chessboard* and the grains of rice that can be used to introduce exponential growth in a classroom. However, Chandra decided to create his own story rather than use an existing one. He explained that his story was inspired by the work of Theonni Pappas (1991), in *More Joy of Mathematics*. According to Pappas, the construction of a Japanese sword was an elaborate and invariable process dominated by pattern. The sword-maker would heat a piece of steel until it was at welding temperature, fold the steel over, weld it, and then forge it to its original dimensions. This process was repeated 22 times, which produced over 4 million layers of steel (Pappas, 1991). This explains why Samurai swords are so light, yet strong enough to cut through even the densest of metals. In what follows we provide the story created by this teacher, as retold by the author (Balakrishnan, 2008). We leave it to the reader to imagine the scenery, the voice and intonation of the teller, the change of pace or tone and the reactions of the audience.

> *Steam rose from the ground as the great warrior rode onto the bloodied field. The smell of raw flesh and guts would cause anyone to curl over and vomit... but not Chikara Ni Bai. He had seen his fair share of death as a Samurai and leader of his people. He was finished fighting now. His only desire was to return home and hold his beloved son in his arms once again. He gathered the other warriors together and began the long journey back to Tengoku No Tani, which means "heaven's valley." Ni Bai was known throughout the land for his skill with the sword. Some say he received this*

CHAPTER 11

gift as a child from the spirits, but Ni Bai knew it was his apprenticeship under his sensei, Gogun Yamaguchi[*] *that had led him to discover the subtle art of sword-handling. Ni Bai thought about all the things he would do with his son...play...tell jokes...play stuff...give him money...all the things a father is supposed to do with an eleven year old boy. As they neared the village, Chacho, the Village Idiot, and apprentice to Ni Bai, who had not yet learned the art of biting one's tongue, let out a blood-curdling yell [wait for one student to yell]. For there, across the meadow rose smoke. It was coming from their village. "My son!" yelled Ni Bai. The whole village had been destroyed. While the warriors, and Chacho, the Village Idiot, had been away, Akuma No Niisan, Ni Bai's one-time apprentice and now mortal enemy, had ravaged the village. Nothing was left...the women had been killed, the men had been carried off, and the animals had all been fixed. Ni Bai ran to his house in the center of the village. There, lying in the doorway was his wife. She had been stabbed. Blood was squirting everywhere. Ni Bai, however, only had one thing on his mind – his son. He ran into his son's room and at once, fell to his knees. There, on the cold wooden floor was his son's body – but no head. Ni Bai fell down beside his son – or at least most of his son – and let out a blood-curdling yell [wait for a student to let out a yell]. Next to his son's body was a piece of rice paper with the words "I have your son's head" written on it. Ni Bai had only one thought, revenge... revenge. But to defeat his mortal enemy, the great Chikara Ni Ba would need help. Not the help of man or beast. No, Ni Bai would need a sword...a sword of great power and speed. There was only one man who could create a sword of this distinction....Jigokubi Hanzo. Hanzo was famous for his sword-making skills. Many believed that the person who carries one of Hanzo's swords will never know defeat. Ni Bai set out immediately for Hanzo's village which was several moons away. When he arrived at Hanzo's home, the door swung open and the sword-maker fell down at the warrior's feet and let out a blood-curdling yell [wait for students to yell]. "Word has come to me that the great Chikara Ni Bai is to avenge the death of his son," Hanzo began. "I know what it is like to lose someone you love. I once lost my father. He was at the grocery store. One minute he was looking at the zucchinis and the next minute he was gone. What's worse, the zucchinis were gone too. Every week they call trying to get me to pay for those zucch...." Ni Bai interrupted, "I have come..." "Wait...I know what you have come for," said Hanzo. "You want a sword. One like no other that has come before it. A sword so deadly, that even the sight of it will bring fear to its enemies. A sword so strong it can cut through the most solid of metals and so light it can move through the air*

---

[*] The reader may note that Gogun Yamaguchi was the founding father of Gojo-ru Karate in Okinawa – the same brand of karate Daniel Laruso learns in *The Karate Kid*. (Chandra's comment)

more swiftly than a greased chicken on a water slide." "You can make a sword of this nature?" asked Ni Bai. "I begin tonight," said Hanzo. That evening, Hanzo took one sheet of steel and placed it in the fire – a fire hotter than the very fires of hell. The steel began to turn red and then blue and then white. Hanzo let out a blood-curdling yell [wait for student] and then let his hammer fall upon the now obedient metal. He hammered it and hammered it putting his very soul into each swing. After some careful maneuvering he folded the metal over, and then beat it into submission. [How many layers are there now? How many folds?]. Again, he took the folded sheet of steel and placed it in the fire...and again he let out a blood-curdling yell [wait for student]. Once again he hammered the naughty piece of steel until it seemed like the life had left it. And again he folded the steel over. [How many layers are there now? How many folds? How many times do you think Hanzo did this process in total?] 21 times the sword-maker punished the steel in this way. [Now how many folds? How many layers?]. After seven days and seven nights, Hanzo emerged from his workshop to present the warrior with the greatest sword he had ever forged. "I give you, 'Tetsu No Tamashi'," said Hanzo. [This means "Iron Spirit"]. Ni Bai took the sword and held it up to the sky. A shimmer of light worked its way up the sword. "Careful, Ni Bai...even looking at this sword can draw blood," said Hanzo. Ni Bai let out a cry of victory, "aaaaaaaaeeeeeiiiiooooooo." He jumped onto his horse and rode off to meet his enemy No Niisan. The warrior knew this would be his greatest battle... Tetsu No Tamashi went before him...

The story incorporates a variety of elements that we discussed in detail in Chapter 2; there is an engaging plot that embeds a mathematical pattern in a suspenseful context, there is a detailed description of scenery that engages imagination, there is a villain and mortal enemy that is cast against a legendary Samurai warrior, and there is conflict and conflict resolution.

In the story the listener follows Ni Bai in his quest to avenge the death of his only son. In designing the plot Chandra sought help of his colleague, a teacher of Japanese, in order to carefully devise names for characters and places in the story that clearly identify their position in the conflict:

Chikara Ni Bai (the great warrior)–"Strength Times 2"
Akuma No Niisan (the evil warlord) –"Devil's Older Brother"
Jigokubi Hanzo (the sword-maker) –"Hellfire Hanzo"
Tengoku No Tani (Ni Bai's village) –"Heaven's Valley"
Ja Aku No Donzoku (No Niisan's village) –"Evil Abyss"
Tetsu No Tamashi (the magical sword) –"Iron Spirit"

Furthermore, the story is designed to emphasize the element of humour via interaction with the audience, a vital element of storytelling that is rather hard to transfer through text.

After telling this story, Chandra asked his students to write stories that involve exponents and exponential growth. Some of these stories are reproduced below.

CHAPTER 11

From Lee

One day I was in my backyard when an alien spaceship came and beamed me up! One alien started poking me with a stick... every second after that, two aliens for each alien that was appeared and started poking me. How many aliens were poking me after one minute? 2^0 2^1 2^2 2^3...

From Julia

It was Halloween night and the children were pouring into my door yelling, "trick or treat, give me something good to eat". So I listened. The first kid came so I gave him 2 candies. Then 2 kids came, I gave them 4 candies in total. Then two kids came and I gave them 8 candies in total. So I wanted to know if I continued on the same streak and if another 2 kids came how much chocolate/candy I would have to give them?

$2^2=4$; $2^3=8$; $2^4=16$

So I would have to give them 16 candies in total and if I continued on the same streak all my candy would be gone quite quickly! I then decided to eat them all. Unfortunately, I was sick the next morning and was rushed to the hospital for hallucinating.

From Corey

There is a man in "New York City" named Bill. Bill opened up a hot dog stand when he was younger. On his very first day of business, Bill sold only 5 hot dogs. On the next day, business got better [and] Bill sold 25 hot dogs. On day three, business got even better [and] Bill sold 125 hot dogs. On the fourth day, business was BOOMING! Bill sold a whopping 625 hot dogs. Bill is now a multi BILIIONAIRE being the creator of Microsoft. After all, his full name is Bill Gates.

Hot Dogs	Repeated Multiplication	Exponents
5	5	5^1
25	5×5	5^2
125	$5 \times 5 \times 5$	5^3
625	$5 \times 5 \times 5 \times 5$	5^4

From Leah

One summer, Adam, Billy, Caroline, Dave and Elizabeth decided to make some money. They applied at the corner store and [they] all got the job. They talked to the owner and instead of just getting paid $5 an hour, each hour they would get higher. Adam worked one hour and got $5. Billy

STORIES OF A TEACHER AND HIS STUDENTS

worked two hours and got $25 and by the time it got to Elizabeth who worked 5 hours, she got paid $3125.

1	5^1
2	5^2
3	5^3
4	5^4
5	5^5

From Bob

Bob was going to throw a small party. There would be 4^2 people at the party including Bob. His first attempt to cook for his guests was a disaster. First the burgers caught fire, igniting his apron and singeing his eyebrows. Now Bob wasn't that smart. Knowing that his guests would be arriving soon, he went to the drawer and got his scissors. He then cut pieces of the hair from his head, and glued them on his forehead where his eyebrows used to be. Now since he used some of his hair for new eyebrows, he had a big bald spot, right in the middle of his head se he decided to wear his hat.

Bob decided to try hotdogs. When the guests arrived, Bob told them that they were going to roast the hot dogs over a bon fire. When Bob was cooking his hotdog, it caught fire, so Bob tried to blow it out. When Bob blew, his hotdog flew into one of the guests' face, which made him bump into another guest and that guest hit another and eventually every one and their hotdogs were lying in a heap on the grass. Bob decided to order pizza. Bob knew that a large pizza had 3^2 slices and a medium had 2^3 slices. He estimates each guest would eat between 2 and 3 slices each. Bob knew he would need to order a minimum of 2 to the fifth power slices and less then 7^2 slices. Bob, who was not very good at math decided to order 3 medium pizzas and 3 large pizzas. He would eat the extra 3 slices for lunch the next day.

From Karoline

One day Mark was going to the store to buy a new shower cap because his old was ripped. The store clerk told him that they were $10 each. Mark spent 10^2. He had $200 with him so he spent ½ of his money. With the rest of the money he bought some goggles. He bought 2 pairs, they each cost $2 he spent 2^2. In the end he had spent a total of $104

From Becky

All the trees in an elementary school's playground were cut down. It looked very bare out there so the school decided to plant a couple of trees in the playground. One of teachers went and bought some seeds for the kids to plant. After the trees were planted, the seeds started to grow. Everyday the trees got lots of sun, because it was during the summer, Fertilizer and some

CHAPTER 11

water which each kid will get to water the tree. Everyday the trees get fertilizer, sunlight and water it would triple in size and after 3 days the seed would start growing into a tree. After 10 days how tall will the tree be?

Tree	Tree getting bigger	Exp. Form
3	1	3^1
3	3	3^2
9	27	3^3
27	81	3^4
81	243	3^5
243	729	3^6
729	2189	3^7
2189	6561	3^8
6561	19683	3^9
1968	59049	3^{10}

3

The tree will be 59049 mm tall after 10 days

From Diana

A long time ago during the prehistoric age, Mr. Balakrishnan and three of his friends decided to have a party. Each person went out and found four friends. But it wasn't big enough for them. They wanted to have as many people as they could to come to their party. So again everybody went out and got four more friends to come. They did this 5 times until they finally thought they had enough people. Unfortunately, after all their hard work, an old woman named Mrs. Whitehead who lived on their street had called the cops and had their party shut down.

How many people were at the party before it was shut down?

4 to the power of 5

4x4x4x4x4= 1024

From Alec

Generic Joe had a generic problem. He needed a generic cloth for generic face-washing time. He decided to visit the generically Abnormal Bob, the only known cloth-maker (not a generic cloth-maker). Abnormal Bob lived abnormally on the abnormal side of town, so Generic Joe needed to travel generically over there. He drove his generic car for a generic while until he reached the abnormal part of town. He stepped into Abnormal Bob's abnormal home. Abnormal Bob asked him about his generic problem. Abnormally, Abnormal Bob had the generic materials to make the generic cloth. In order to make a generic cloth, the generic materials have to be twisted 7 times, then hardened with generic starch, and then softened with

STORIES OF A TEACHER AND HIS STUDENTS

generic fabric softener. The generic cloth is done when Abnormal Bob has done this 11 times.

$7^{11} = 1,977,326,743$

There are 1,977,326,743 twists.

From Hanna

T'was a warm evening in the middle of August and the children of the village were putting on their costumes for trick or treating. You might ask why they were trick or treating in August, but that shall forever remain a mystery. Back to the story, Xavier and his four friends, Zolt, Heath, Lief and MPLZ3 were approaching the house that had the MAGIC GUMBALL MACHINE!!! The owners of the house were in fact very lazy on Halloween so they installed a fantastic self-serve gumball machine into their front door. (9 easy payments of 99$.) Xavier was first to his gumball. He turns the knob... and (gasp here) 13 pukey green gumballs roll out. Leif skips up to the fantastic gumball machine and receive 169 mustard yellow gumballs.

"AYE BANANAS!" says Zolt. Why do get so many?

"HOTDOGS" says MPLZ3.

"WHAT?" asks Zolt

"never mind"

Anyway, how many gumballs should Zolt get if he were to go next, and how many would MPLZ3 get after Zolt?

People	#of Gumballs	Exponents	Repeated Multiplication
Xavier	13	13	13
Lief	169	13^2	13×13
Zolt	2197	13^3	$13 \times 13 \times 13$
MPLZ3	28561	13 to the 4	$13 \times 13 \times 13 \times 13$

In the end Xavier was very jealous of how much candy his friends.

Too bad Xavier ☹

From Brian

There was a kid named Sid who decided to mow people's lawns every month. So Sid asked a guy named Fly if he could mow his lawn every month. Fly said sure and that he would pay Sid double the salary of the previous month. Fly gave him 3 dollars the first month. Sid wondered how much his salary would be on the 12th month.

CHAPTER 11

Month	Salary
1	*$3*
2	*$9*
3	*$27*
4	*$81*
5	*$243*
6	*$729*
...	*...*
10	*$59049*
11	*$117147*
12	*$531441*

He would get $531, 441.

3^{12} or 531441. Fly is crazy!

From Cassidy

Our school together a cheerleading group. We needed to raise money for the uniforms. To raise money, we decided to do bottle drives every second weekend. The first time we did the bottle drive 3 people showed up. In all, that day we made $10.00. Two weeks later we got together again. This time 12 people showed up. The total for that was 10 times the amount from the first time. The third time we did a bottle drive the whole team cam. That day we made the most money yet. We had made 10 times the amount we had made at the second bottle drive. If we needed $1500 for the uniform did we make enough to pay for them? If not, what is the difference?

From Gemma

The students of Birchwood High gathered in the lunchroom. As always, competition lingered in the air. It could nearly suffocate you and being with this 'group' –though only seven students – kept you on your toes all the time. Maria glanced around nervously, she had been drawn into this so-called group through her own will of being noticed, feeling the temptation of winning. Yes, this was the Birchwood High dare council. Only those driven by competition could complete one of these dares. For a while no one spoke, they only looked at one another, through threatening eyes. Every one looked now at the leader. He would name the dare, eventually. It could be anything, last week it got three people suspended. At last the leader spoke. Maria cast her head down in embarrassment. What had she gotten herself into?

"A fool would name one single dare, therefore mine progresses throughout the five days of the week. Think carefully before quickly accepting the challenge. Consequences could be 'bigger' than suspension. A generous prize will be rewarded, of course," he added with a smirk. This leader wasn't the nicest student, but he was bright and knew how pride could draw people into the most foolish situations.

Maria let her mind wander. "I wonder what sort of prize this might be, it could be anything. This leader is rich and if I did this dare I could be recognized, forever!"

"Let me name the dare" the leader said. All eyes shot up once again to him.

"As you know, the Birchwood High cafeteria has a large quantity of delicious hamburgers. Mouth watering ones. Big juicy ones."

"Hamburgers?" thought Maria. "What sort of dare was that? I thought that I might have to do something at lest remotely daring. How easy!" but her thoughts were interrupted with the leader again.

"Starting on the first day of the week the victim will eat two hamburgers." he said. The others in the group started to laugh. "What kind of dare is this?" someone shouted out. "All we need to do is eat hamburgers?!"

The leader smiled, "There's a bit of a catch" he said, "Every day of the week the hamburgers double in numbers and you must eat every one, to the last crumb. Any takers? Or will I pick someone myself?"

Maria, before calculating the total consumption number, shot up her hand before anyone else could. Her mouth was watering and to complete the dare would bring her popularity in the school, or so he hoped.

The leader smiled. "Thank you Maria, if you complete the dare the prize is yours."

The next day Maria ate two huge juicy hamburgers. To her she tasted only her own greed for the prize and the recognition that came with it. Over the course of the next several days she found her diet hugely increasing. She was feeling heavier and more grotesque by the day. And when on the third day and eating eight burgers she questioned her decision.

By the end of the dare session, she had gained exactly what she had wanted. To be noticed, and now weighing the mass of many burgers she was indeed noticed. Her dream was achieved. She would be forever noticed and the dare had turned out to be very big indeed. After doubling the burgers every day she finished the week having eaten 62 hamburgers finishing the last day with 32.

From Andrew

One morning I woke up. Except this morning I woke up differently. I thought I don't want to go to school today. So I called a cab and left my house to go to the airport (don't you wish you could do that). When I was at

CHAPTER 11

the airport I thought 'cool I'm at the airport and I'm not at school. Hahahahaah' So I got out of the cab but I didn't have any money to pay the driver. "Excuse me sir, you have to pay me" said the dim- witter driver. I said "I don't have any money I guess you'll have to drive me back." The guy said Okay. I said "but don't worry, I'll let you go without having to drive me." The driver said "oh thanks buddy I owe you one." Idiot. Then he drove away. I entered the place and went to get my ticket. In a matter of minutes, I was on my one-way flight to Paris, France. It took a while so I napped and snoozed and dozed and slumbered and slept the whole way there. When I got there, I went to a bread-making place and got a scrumptious French Baguette. My bread and I decided to go to the Eiffel Tower. So we did. It costs money to get up there (can you believe it) so I decided to use my super teleporter thing-ga-ma-jig to get up there. It was exactly .072 seconds. Trust me, I counted. I read a plaque up there it was in Japanese and it said that the builders used the math to build the tower. As I was reading, by mistake I dropped my bread and it hit some hobo. Stupid butter. Anyways, exactly 33,554,432 metal triangles were used to build it. For each triangle they used they had to double that the next layer on the way down (they actually built the tower from top to bottom). If I wasn't in Mr. B's class, I would not find any math in this method. But I am so I understand that the architects used the exponents instead of repeated multiplication. The builders ended up with a massive, giant, big, large, huge, enormously gigantic square based pyramid. Then those Frenchie's used their baguette knives to cut out the middle of the tower and shaped it so that it was aerodynamically designed. Anyways back to math. There were 26 layers of triangles in the whole tower. If the layers were started at 1 and went down, and the triangles doubled for each layer, it would equal to 33, 554, 432 triangles. If in the second layer there are 2 triangles, then in the third layer there would be 4. if you repeat this process until the twenty sixth layer, you should have 33,554,432 triangles. The equation would be 2 to the power of 25.

From Brent

This is a story about what happens when you eat chips when you're on a diet. First you'll say that your only going to have just one. Then you have one and its so good that you think, well maybe 2 more wont hurt. Then they're so good that you decide they're not that fattening and have 4 more. And they're soo good that you look at the package that says 100g sunflower oil and you think that that means they're good for you, so you have 8 more. And they're soooo good that you figure you've been working sooo hard that you deserve this and eat 16 more chips. She keeps making excuses until she explodes and her family sues the chip company for making their chips so good.

What do we find in students' stories?

First, and likely the most important element of this exercise is in creating opportunity for students to do something different, to open the door for their artistic expression and break the stigma of a standard mathematical drill. While some students wrote simple and short stories to satisfy the teacher's assignment (e.g. Lee, Diana), other engaged their imaginations and creative powers (e.g. Gemma, Andrew, Hanna).

For a teacher, students' stories provide a clear indication of students' understanding and can serve as an assessment instrument. For example, there is a clear indication in the stories of Lee, Julia and Corey that they have a solid grasp of the pattern of the exponential growth. On the other hand, the stories of Bob and Karoline show lack of such understanding.

Further indication of students' understanding is in their ability to provide a variation – while the story designed by Chandra used 2 as the base of the exponent, several students varied the value of the base, using numbers 3, 4, 5, 7, or 13. This shows that they were not 'stuck on doubling', but were able to extend the pattern to include other bases. What is also interesting to note is that some stories that involve exponential growth end up with relatively small numbers, such as 32 or 2^5 hamburgers that Maria had to eat or $16=2^4$ candies given out at Halloween, while other stories take advantage of the powers of a hand held calculator, such as $59049 = 3^{10}$ millimetres the height of a rapidly growing tree or $1,977,326,743 = 7^{11}$ twists in a generic cloth.

While some stories present rather simple scenarios or "barebones" plots, others involve a variety of literary components, involving personal creativity and an attempt to mimic what was introduced by the teacher. We find in students' stories mystery and humour, conflict and imagery. What is interesting to note from the perspective of teaching mathematics, is that the majority of work produced by the students involved not only the story, but also the solution of a problem presented in a story, though this was not an explicit requirement of the task. In several places the pattern was presented in a table to help the exposition, in other places only a numerical solution appeared.

EPISODE 2: STORIES THAT ACCOMPANY

In order to attract students' interest towards the chapter on irrational numbers Chandra told them the classical story about the Pythagoreans, their strange beliefs and behaviours, and their fear when the discovery of irrational numbers was made. Students were introduced to the secret organization of Pythagoreans, their cult of numbers and their notion that 'everything is number', meaning that everything can be measured with whole numbers or a ratio of whole numbers. They were further introduced to a conflict presented by Hippasos of Metapontum in the discovery that the side and diagonal of a square are incommensurable, that is, cannot be measured with the same unit. This meant that if a side of a square is a rational number, its diagonal cannot be represented as a ratio of whole numbers. That is, it is irrational.

CHAPTER 11

The discovery was damaging to the Pythagoreans' belief in mathematical symmetry and so they attempted to conceal it. The legend says that Pythagoreans threw Hippasos into the sea in an attempt to preserve their belief in the harmony of numbers.

Chandra asked his students to implement their understanding of the events described in the legend in creating plays or songs. We reproduce several examples below. Our first example is the chorus from one of the many humorous songs students wrote and performed:

> *We will worship numbers and believe they are Gods,*
> *Meditate and talk to their brains.*
> *7, 8, and 9, and 10, and evens and odds,*
> *We'll love them 'till none others remain.*
>
> *Aliens intelligent, and can't be outdone,*
> *I'm an alien 'cause I'm the smartest one.*
> *Lastly we'll be vegetarians, and no beans,*
> *No meat for us, just give us our greens.*

Our next example is a script written by a group of students who decided to set their play within the context of a news team reporting on the recovered body of Hippasos.

> ANCHOR: *The gruesome discovery of a drowned body was reported today in the island of Samos. Our own Eugene L. Peterson Waddlesworth the Third has gone to find out more. Eugene?*
>
> REPORTER: *Yes, Kent?*
>
> ANCHOR: *Can you tell us anything of the police's discoveries so far?*
>
> REPORTER: *Well, Kent, several chains with metal balls were found wrapped around the body, as well as heavy rocks in the pockets and cement blocks on its feet, as if to make sure it would sink. The police, for some reason, are suspecting foul play.*
>
> ANCHOR: *(Dripping with sarcasm) How did they figure that?*
>
> REPORTER: *(absolutely serious) No idea, Kent.*
>
> ANCHOR: *O...kay...(startled by the ignorance) So...what else is going on down there?*
>
> REPORTER: *All the police members have declined requests for interviews...however, there are some locals near the crime site. Let me talk to one of them.*
>
> *(Goes over to a suspicious looking local, wearing shades and looking around)*
>
> REPORTER: *Excuse me, sir, but would you mind if I asked you some questions?*

LOCAL: *Questions? What kind of questions?*

REPORTER: *I see you're wearing a unique sweater! (reads off it)*

The - secret - society - of - Pythagoras. Does this mean, and I don't mean to jump to conclusions in any way, that you indeed belong to a secret society?

LOCAL: *What? Who told you that?*

REPORTER: *Well, sir, it's on your sweater.*

LOCAL: *You've got nothing on me, you hear? NOTHING!*

(Runs away twitching)

As in the previously described students' stories, the plays students wrote displayed various degrees of engagement with the mathematical content. While some students simply repeated the legend, others incorporated their understanding of the mathematical content. Consider another excerpt from the above news report:

REPORTER: *What's that, constable?*

CONSTABLE: *This? I think it's a litter box. (gives it to reporter)*

REPORTER: *There's some stuff on this.*

CONSTABLE: *Well, obviously.*

REPORTER: *No, no, there are little sticks! It looks like they are arranged into some shape.*

CONSTABLE: *Looks like half a square.*

ANCHOR: *You mean like that? (holds up a picture of half a square)*

REPORTER: *Yeah. The base has three sticks ...*

CONSTABLE: *The height is four sticks and five sticks connecting them.*

ANCHOR: *So it's a right triangle made of sticks?*

REPORTER: *Yeah.*

(Anchor arranges sticks into a right triangle)

REPORTER: *And there are squares here, too.*

ANCHOR: *What do you mean?*

CONSTABLE: *There are three squares.*

REPORTER: *Each of their sides are one of the sides of the right triangle.*

ANCHOR: *(puts on more sticks) Like this?*

CONSTABLE: *Yeah.*

ANCHOR: *Hey, I think I've seen this before. This is actually something Pythagoras found out. This square (the one with side 4) has the area of*

CHAPTER 11

> 16. And this square (the one with side 3) has the area of nine, while this side (5) has the area of 25.
>
> CONSTABLE: What's that got to do with anything?
>
> ANCHOR: It's quite interesting. If you add the area of this square (16) and this square (9)...
>
> REPORTER: It's the area of the other square!
>
> CONSTABLE: Here's another one of those litter boxes.
>
> REPORTER: The shape on this is a lot smaller than the other one.
>
> ANCHOR: What does it look like?
>
> REPORTER: Well, the shape is exactly the same as the other one, except its height and base is only one stick.
>
> ANCHOR: (after arranging it) Wait, but how many sticks is the other side?
>
> REPORTER: There are two sticks, but they don't fit in perfectly into that side.
>
> (silence)
>
> CONSTABLE: I don't think a whole number of sticks can fit in there.
>
> REPORTER: Yeah.
>
> ANCHOR: What? But what about the squares?
>
> REPORTER: What about them?
>
> ANCHOR: Well, if we can't get the exact value of this side, how can we have a square?
>
> CONSTABLE: Erm.

Another play described the interaction between Hippasus and Pythagoras:

> PYTHAGORAS: Do you want to join our cult, and worship Numbers?
>
> HIPPASUS: Yes, I'd be honoured!
>
> PYTHAGORAS: Well you're in Hippopotamus.
>
> P, F, & H: Numbers numbers numbers numbers numbers numbers numbers numbers...
>
> NARRATOR: "So the group prays and studies for years until one day, while they are on a Greek warship, sailing in the formation of a square, one of the warships sinks!
>
> PYTHAGORAS: Hippopotamus, we need you to do a calculation for us.
>
> FOLLOWER: We hang ropes of equal length in between each ship so that they stay in perfect formation. Since one of the ships has sunk; we need

you to find out the length of rope required to connect the two now unattached ships.

Each rope is one unit, so we'll leave you to figure out how much rope we'll need.

HIPPASUS: One thing before you go, my name is Hippasus...

P & F: Right...

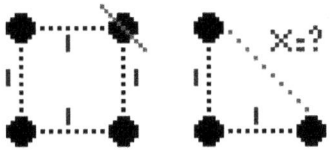

NARRATOR: So Hippasus meditates on the problem, but figures out that he can't get a perfect numeral, and he then figures out that numbers are not perfect...

HIPPASUS: Hey, guys, guess what, I found out that numbers are not perfect! The number that I got for the amount of rope that we need is not a whole number, but a decimal that goes on and on!

H&F: Oh no, what, no way, blasphemy, lies...

PYTHAGORAS: We can't tolerate this, he is speaking blasphemy against us and Apollo!

FOLLOWER: Let's throw him overboard!

What is there in students' work?

Yet again, in addition to all the possible benefits of creative endeavour, we suggest that students' scripts provide the teacher with a good idea of their understanding. For example, in the news report students implement their understanding of the Pythagorean Theorem by determining the number of sticks needed for a diagonal. In the situation created in the last play the task becomes embedded in the context – the need is not simply to calculate the length of a diagonal in a square, but to find out the amount of rope needed to attach two ships. Students implemented their understanding by creating an isomorphic and realistic model.

However, students also demonstrated a possible confusion between whole numbers and rational numbers. The confusion surfaces in having Hippasus declare "I found out that numbers are not perfect! The number that I got for the amount of rope that we need is not a whole number" and, similarly, having the constable claim "I do not think a whole number of sticks can fit in here". It may be possible that the above claims attributed to Hippasus or the constable are meant to be the characters' misunderstandings rather than their own. Either way it opens a wonderful route for a teacher to pursue.

CHAPTER 11

EPISODE 3: STORY THAT ASKS A QUESTION

In Chapter 8 we mentioned that any 'standard' word problem can be turned into a story. In what follows we show how Chandra implements this idea. The problem he wanted his students to work on is a problem of uniform motion or rate of work.

A standard problem of this kind may appear as follows:

> *A plane leaves Vancouver heading for Toronto travelling at a rate of 200 km/h. One hour later, another plane leaves Vancouver heading for Toronto at a rate of 300 km/h. How long before the second plane catches up to the first plane?*

This is a fairly simple problem to solve, but like most word problems found in textbooks, it lacks any emotional appeal. Chandra redressed the problem, bringing the context close to students in a vivid and humorous fashion.

> *Carey and Brian* [Actual students' names were used] *decided they were going to skip math class today, as they were tired from the party last night. "Hey dude, let's go to the mall where all the cool people hang out"* [spoken in a stereotypical California surfer voice]. *"Sounds like a plan dude!" So Carey and Brian headed out on foot for the mall at 8:30 am travelling at a rate of 10 km/h. Well, Mr. B. realized Carey and Brian were not in class, and asked the other students where they were. Tina [another student in class] ratted them out and told Mr. B. they were heading to the mall. Of course, considering Mr. B. is in top shape and a world-class speed-walker, he also set out on foot but travelling at a rate of 25 km/h. Before he could leave however, it took Mr. B. 30 minutes to put on his spandex pants. What time did Mr. B. catch up to Carey and Brian and penalize them for skipping class?*

Chandras' personalization of characters, humour, as well as a context close to students' lives creates the appeal in this story.

EPISODE 4: STORY TO INTRODUCE AN ACTIVITY

The Murder Mystery story was created by Chandra to engage his students in exploring linear equations. An activity was set in the context of a murder mystery and students were the 'detectives' in charge of tracking down a serial killer. The students were put into groups and handed a 'secret envelope'. Inside the envelope were floor plans of the school with Cartesian graphs superimposed on them and a letter that said the following:

> *You have been given the task of tracking down a criminal – me. My crime will be revealed in time, but for now, you will have to use your mathematical prowess in a way you never dreamed. To find me, you will have to carefully solve the following clues using the maps of the school. You may want to bring a ruler and pencils along too! Make sure you keep your work as proof of your skills – otherwise you will surely fail.*

STORIES OF A TEACHER AND HIS STUDENTS

Graph on the lower floor map the linear equation that passes through the point (8,-10) and has a slope of 2. Then on the same map graph the linear equation that passes through the point (10,-9) and has an undefined slope. The intersection of these two lines is your destination. If you hurry you will catch me.

Chandra explained that his inspiration for this activity came from a particular scene in the novel, *Angels and Demons* by Dan Brown (Brown, 2000), in which the main character, Robert Langdon, determines a point on a map based on the outline of a cross formed by the location of four churches.

Experiencing significant success with this activity, as indicated by students' engagement, Chandra decided to create a variation. Rather than having students follow the clues, he wanted them to create their own clues in order to describe locations on the map. This is a task on a higher level of sophistication. To achieve this goal, Chandra created a new story, Skull Island, that involved pirates, violence, and a treasure hunt.

It was 15 years to the day when I first saw that cursed map. The woman at the counter had watched me from the moment I walked into the curio shop. It wasn't until I picked up the map and started to examine it that she stumbled over to me and touched my hand. "You are the map-bearer," she said in her thick Jamaican accent. "She's obviously crazy," I thought. But something compelled me to believe her. This was no ordinary map...superimposed on it was a Cartesian coordinate grid – not the regular latitude and longitude lines! There were a few lines that appeared to have been drawn... in blood?!! Written over each line seemed to be markings that resembled linear equations [students laugh]. This was quite possible as the date on the map was 1698 AD – only years after Descartes developed his graphing system. I tried to give the map back to her, but she wouldn't let me. She pushed my hand away and then...right in front of me...she dropped dead! Did I cause her death...or was it that cursed map? I knew something was different about it. Sprawled across the top of the map were the words "Skull Island." A cold shiver went up my spine – almost felt like a hook or a dagger against my back! Okay, my imagination was getting away from me. What was very real however, was that on the map was a big red "X". I knew what that meant – treasure! After all the chaos following the woman's death had passed, I quickly went to meet my friends in the hotel and show them the map. We tried for several days to find out where the island on the map was located, and how we might go there, but none of the locals seemed willing to talk to us after seeing the map. They were scared – as if they had seen a ghost! "What evil had forged this document?" I wondered. The only option was to go to the library and see if we could find out more about this "Skull Island." Our persistence paid off – well, as much as evil and death and revenge is a good thing...you see, the map was made by the most evil of pirates – the legendary "Bloodhead"! Very little was written about this depraved buccaneer. Apparently, he was

CHAPTER 11

the most feared of pirates. Legend has it that Bloodhead was so evil, when some locals kidnapped his wife and children in order to get some of his booty, Bloodhead burst into the home of the kidnappers and shot and killed... his entire family – leaving the kidnappers alive! He was noted as saying, "I would rather see them dead a thousand times over than to have them come between me and my gold." To this day, no one utters the name of Bloodhead... unless they wish a curse upon them... Bloodhead... Bloodhead... Bloodhead...

As mentioned above, it was the students' task to create a map and identify the route of the pirate and location of treasure using linear equations. Having completed the task, the students exchanged their 'clues' is a search of each others hidden treasure.

The context of a treasure hunt inspired students to create their own story-activities that integrate clues in the form of linear equations. We share with the reader several excerpts from one such story:

Welcome to the world of Shrek. This is a once and a lifetime opportunity. You get a chance to win the Shrek prize. But the question is, are you up for the challenge? To make it more fun, you and your partner can be in character. You and your partner can decide of who will be playing the role of Shrek and who will be Shreks sidekick Donkey! But remember, you don't have to. Now before you begin I will go over some rules.

First rule: NO CHEATING

Second Rule: Must show all your work

Third rule: Every time you find a location, come and see us and we will give you the rest of the story bit by bit.

Fourth Rule: You must read the story that comes with it and when you find where the new location is, come to us and we will give you another piece of the story and two more equations.

Fifth Rule: HAVE FUN!

Now begin your brilliant journey!

Oh it was a hot, gruesome day. Shrek was so bored. Not only was it hot, but Fiona had left to visit her parents at Far Far Away Kingdom by herself. It wasn't that Shrek wasn't invited, but it was Parent Day and Fiona wanted to spend some quality time with her parents. "Oh Donkey, why must you stay with me? Don't you have any parents you can annoy ... I mean visit?" Donkey replied happily, "Yes, but they happened to go far away on vacation for two days". Shrek rolled his eyes. "Don't you think it's a little strange how they chose to go on vacation right before Parent Day on the last minute?" asked Shrek. Donkey stood there and pondered for a brief second and then just shook his head, "Nope." All of a sudden Donkey had a

STORIES OF A TEACHER AND HIS STUDENTS

great idea. He told Shrek of this treasure map he found. Shrek didn't want to go but Donkey wouldn't stop talking so he agreed. They left from Shrek's Swamp and that's where their journey began. The first hints (equations) on the map are....

With slope -1 and y-intercept 13 (for one line)

With slope -0 and y-intercept 14 (for another line)

Good job you guys found the next location. Shrek and Donkey have just arrived at the abandoned Farquuad's Castle. Shrek was feeling uneasy about the place so they both tried to find the clue as fast as they could so they could get out of that place. They were lucky because they found a guard who was wearing a shirt with an equation like thing. They thought that, that couldn't possibly be it but there was nothing else. So they wrote down the equation and ran because the guard started chasing them.

Passing through the point (0,10) and parallel to $y = 1x+10$.

With the same y-intercept as $y=-4x+3$ and perpendicular to $=7x+4$.

It turned out that the equation was right. Shrek and Donkey were happy because they didn't want to go back there again. They just arrived at the Dragon's Lair. This is what changed Shreks and Donkeys life forever. Donkey was happy to see Dragon and his little babies. This was really his home but now and then, he visits Shrek. Before they walked in the castle to say hello they saw an equation engraved on the door.

Passing through (0,-9) and parallel to the line which passes through points (6, 2) and (17, -4).

Passing through (0, -6) and perpendicular to the line which passes through (-5, -3) and (6, -6)

Shrek and Donkey have just arrived at the enormous sunflower field. This is where Fiona and he ran around, holding hands for a long time. For Fiona, Shrek grabbed some of the sunflowers to give her later. While Shrek and Donkey were walking around the sunflower field, they noticed that there was one part that had no sunflowers. There in the dirt was two equations written. They are...

With the same x-intercept as the line $5x - y + 7 = 0$ and parallel to the line $7x - y + 9 = 0$

With the same x-intercept as the line $8x - y + 9 = 0$ and perpendicular to the line $-8x - y + 2 = 0$

Their next destination was a scary one for Donkey. They had just reached the Gingerbread House. On the way there Shrek was telling Donkey the Hansel and Gretel story but twisted the ending around. He said that at the end the witch lived and succeeded in eating Hansel and Gretel. Donkey was

CHAPTER 11

so scared that he decided to leave this one for Shrek. Shrek laughed and rolled his eyes. This was the exact gingerbread house that Fiona and he went to for their honeymoon. It looked beautiful. He went to knock on the door and an old, ugly lady came and gave him a note. It gave him the equations. They are...

Passing through the points (5, -6) and (12, -3)

Passing through the points (7, -6) and (4, -8)

Shrek and Donkey have arrived at a place they have never been to before, The Palace of Aladdin. When they walked in the palace Shrek had to pull Donkey the whole way because Donkey wouldn't stop flirting with Jasmine and Aladdin was getting a bit angry.

Then they come upon a magic lamp and Donkey rubbed it. Then a Genie pops up. He says that he'll grant them 3 wishes. Before Shrek could reply, Donkey said food and more food. Shrek quickly blurted out, "We want the equations." Shrek said it fast enough so the Genie gave them food, more food and the equations. They are....

Passing through (-5, 8) with slope – 1

Passing through the point (0, -9) and perpendicular to the line with the equation $3x + y - 9 = 0$

The next destination was another place where Shrek had to pull Donkey along. But not for the beautiful Princess Belle but for the Prince who lived there since Donkey annoyed him. Their destination was Beast's Castle. Shrek understood how the prince felt since the prince seemed to be in a beastly form. The Beast didn't like them walking around his castle at first but the sweet Belle persuaded him to let them. They walked around for an hour or two and finally bumped into Lumière and Clocksworth. They were talking items. They took them to the library and showed them a book with two equations written in them. They are...

Passing through the point (0, -3) and parallel to the line with the equation $6x + y + 3 = 0$

Passing through the origin and perpendicular to the line $11x + y = 0$

Comprehension Questions

1) Who found the treasure map?

2) What two Disney palaces/castles did they go to?

3) Where was the treasure the whole time and who saw the X that was there but didn't tell the other person?

STORIES OF A TEACHER AND HIS STUDENTS

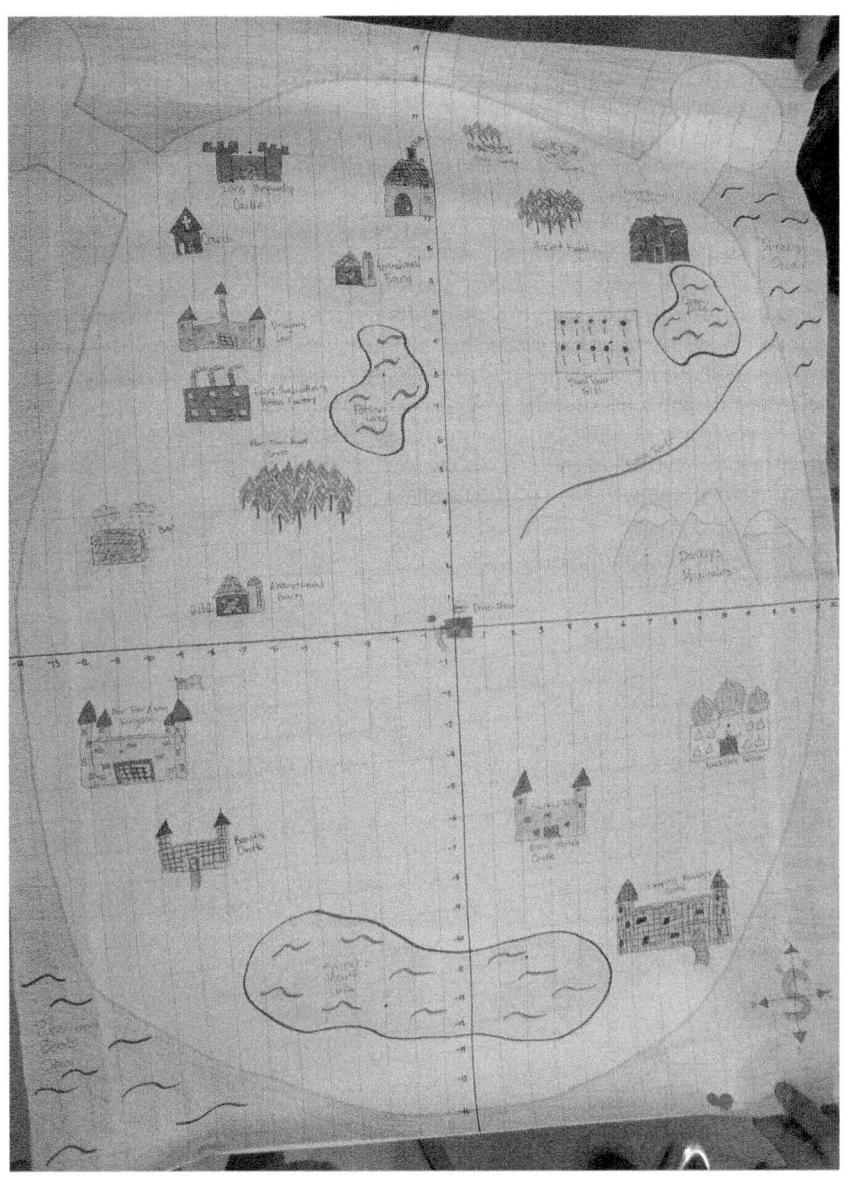

CHAPTER 11

SUMMARY AND A WARNING

Modelling, or demonstration of a way to be followed, is an important part of teaching. In mathematics classrooms, modelling activities often take the shape of so-called 'worked examples', where a teacher introduces an algorithm, method, or a strategy and students imitate the implementation on a different but similar task, either mimicking exactly what was demonstrated or, where necessary, generating a minor variation. In Chandra's class another dimension was added – the teacher's stories served not only as a valuable tool to engage students with mathematics, but also as a model for creativity, humour, and fun.

However, all this does not go without warning. While for many students story-supported work served to enhance their mathematics, some students were either distracted by the context or intentionally used stories as a refuge from mathematics. Their story assignments focused on extensive literary design and creative writing, while disregarding or totally abandoning the mathematical task. Awareness of this danger requires careful attention from the teacher in encouraging imaginative story design, while keeping a clear focus on a mathematical content.

CHAPTER 12

USING EXISTING STORIES

There is a difference between creating a story and telling a story. When the story to be told is not our own that difference grows. This is why in this book we have advocated strongly for teachers to acquire the skills to write their own stories for their own purposes. There are affordances that come with such skills, affordances that may be lost when using existing stories. But these losses can be minimized, and even eliminated, if a greater awareness of the skills inherent in setting up a story is first established. When we create a story we do more than just writing a story – we custom fit a story. That is, we create our stories to satisfy some particular need or to achieve a particular goal, and we tailor our story towards that need or goal. In so doing we layer our story with implicit affordances that will allow us to *teach* with our story as opposed to just *read* our story. This is not a subtle difference. Our goal in this book has not been to just provide the readers with a ready set of stories with which mathematics students can be entertained. In fact, we have deliberately stayed clear of this. Our goal for this book has been to help the readers develop the ability to create their own stories, stories that can elucidate and illuminate mathematics, engage and motivate students, and transform the classroom and teaching. However, in doing so it is essential not only to provide the most central of tools – the story – but also to elaborate upon the skills necessary to use it in teaching mathematics. These skills are assumed (subsumed) in our work on writing/creating stories, implicit in the custom fitting of a story to a pedagogical need or goal. They are part of the fabric of what makes a self-authored story. Being aware of these implicit skills enables teachers to use existing stories in the teaching of mathematics more effectively. Thus, in what follows we first make explicit these skills and then discuss how to capitalize on these skills when selecting and using existing stories in a mathematics classroom.

PURPOSE

When we write a story we start with a purpose in mind. That is, we write a story for a reason. This reason can range from something as simplistic as a desire to entertain our students to something as sophisticated as wishing to provide a context and the impetus for our students to discover a specific mathematical relationship. Regardless of our purpose, however, it is this purpose that grounds our story and provides the underpinnings of all the details and accessories we add to our story.

Often the outcomes that we focus on are curricular outcomes such as some particular mathematics content. For example, in our story of Kathy's outfits in Chapter 8 we were focused on the content of the *Fundamental Principle of*

CHAPTER 12

Counting and we used the story structure to facilitate its introduction. Likewise, in Chapter 7 we introduced the story of the King and his 12 Diamonds to explain the notion of division by zero. From the story of Gauss and his evil (yet oafish) school teacher who inadvertently introduces us to the notion of arithmetic series, to the confused tailor and his struggles with division by a fraction, to Archimedes and his good friend Bartholomew who teach us about circle measurement, we have seen many instances of stories that focus on elucidating a specific mathematics concept.

But not all curricular outcomes are necessarily focused on such specific content. Curriculum is also concerned with global ideas such as pattern recognition, problem solving and one-to-one correspondence, among others. For example, our story of the changing temperature in Chapter 7 is a story that relies on, and draws attention to, the role of patterns in exploring and solving mathematical problems. Patterns were also central to helping Gauss sum up the numbers from 1 to 100, figuring out how many jars there were inside of the story of *Anno's Mysterious Multiplying Jar*, and how much rice was needed for the last square of the *King's Chessboard*. The concept of one-to-one correspondence arises in many places in mathematics with our first introduction to it being the relationship between the number of objects in a set (its cardinality) and the chant of counting the set. We caught a glimpse of this in our story of the shepherd responsible for ensuring that all the sheep returned at night. These examples, among others, deal not with the micro-concepts that we find in the pages of a mathematics textbook, but about the more global (macro) aspects of mathematics.

The development of habits of mind is also an important aspect of the teaching and learning of mathematics. These habits are the glue that hold mathematics together, the universally transferable and applicable notions that enable us to take what we have learned in one context and use it in another. Problem-solving strategies, thought processes, and perseverance are but a few of the characteristics of doing mathematics that we have encountered thus far in this book. When we met the riddle of the missing dollar in Chapter 7 we saw how varying the parameters of a problem can light the way to a solution, a useful strategy in many situations. One of our many encounters with Archimedes taught us about the power of deep thought while another taught us the benefits of perseverance. Through these stories we are striving to bring to our students a piece of what it means to be truly mathematical.

SCRIPT

When we create a story for the purpose of teaching mathematics one of the things that we implicitly write into that story is how we intend to use it to achieve our purpose. That is, when we write a story we also create a particular script for how that story will be utilized in our classroom. We have ultimate control over that script, and as we envision that script we fit the story around it. For example, we may wish to address a particular concept through pattern generation, pattern recognition, and pattern extension. Such a wish can be realized with a story that introduces to the students the initial elements of the pattern. This is a relatively easy task to accomplish. More challenging is the step of pattern recognition, which requires a more active involvement on the part of the students. So, to facilitate this involvement our script would call for a period of student activity, perhaps in small groups, wherein they seek to discover the inherent pattern. This aspect of our script would then be written into our story in the form of a question (or a call to action). Likewise, the final step of pattern extension also requires a period of student activity. Interspersed within these periods of activities can be repeated returns to the story wherein the students' findings are confirmed by the characters in the story.

What is interesting here is the relationship between the script that we envision for how we will use our story and the story itself. When we are crafting our own story these two aspects become intertwined, each indistinguishable from the other. Our story lives inside of our script. However, our script is not always recognizable within our story. Our vision of how the story will be used does not live entirely within its text. To see this let us return to Karl Friedrich Gauss and Mr. Schmidtsenburgersnoff who we first met in Chapter 2. In the conclusion of this particular story a set of questions are posed to Karl's class and then, through the final prompt of the story, to our own class. Here it is clear what the story writers (us) had in mind in terms of class activity when we concluded this story. We had in our script a plan for the class to use the algorithm that Karl created to explore some other problems.

Not all aspects of our script for this story are as explicit, however. In our own use of this story we always pause after Karl blurts out the answer to the original challenge. We pause in order to allow the significance of what Karl had done to sink in, to give our own students a chance to marvel at his brilliance, and to ponder about the accuracy and, perhaps, the source of his solution. This pause is a moment of interaction with our students, and depending on their reaction, we can extend it into conversation or invitation for exploration. Regardless of how we use it, however, this pause is prominent in our script, but it exists in the story only as a paragraph break. It is explicit within our script but implicit within our story.

The same is true for many of the stories that we write. We have attempted to, as much as possible, make these explicit-implicit gaps as transparent as possible. It is from this process that the categorization of stories emerged. Stories that introduce, stories that accompany, stories that intertwine, stories that explain, are all just explications of scripts.

TELLING

Something that we cannot entirely script, however, is the telling of a story. As much as we can plan how we will use a story for the teaching of mathematics, we cannot completely predict how such an endeavour will turn out. The telling of a story is a conversation, a conversation between the storyteller and the audience. In even the most general of storytelling settings it is up to the storyteller to read the audience and to work with the audience to maximize their engagement. When using stories to teach mathematics the same is true – except that, in this context, engagement has some very specific connotations.

As discussed in Chapter 3, the telling of a story is much more than the simple reading of a story. It requires a sense of timing, a sense of presence, and a sense of humour. It requires voice fluctuations, body language, gestures, and eye contact. And it requires audience participation. None of these aspects live within the words of the story. Like the script, these aspects live within the intentions of the story writer. Unlike the script, however, they are much more situational, depending on the audience and the context and the teller's ability to read the mood and needs of individual audience members as well as the audience as a whole.

Our story of the Farmer and the Crow in Chapter 3 showcases how we recruit ideas from the students and incorporate those ideas into our story. In so doing, however, the story is presented much more like a script than as a typical story. But it is more than a script; it is a fictional transcription of one telling of the story. In this transcription details of some of the interactions involved in the telling of the story are present. But we cannot present every story in such a manner.

CONTEXT

When we tell a story we engage our students in the details of the characters, the setting, and the plot. We fill them with a sense of human meaning, wonder, and curiosity. We involve our students in the conflict, the problem to be solved, and the dilemma to be resolved. We draw our students into the context, align them with the characters and include them in the story. In so doing we invite our student to think *about* the story.

But in so doing we also invite our students to think *with* the story. This is different. It is through the emersion in the story that we are able to situate their work, their thoughts, and their solutions. This gives us, as storywriters and storytellers, the ability to use stories for teaching mathematics. Consider again the story of Karl and Mr. Schmidtsenburgersnoff. When the students are set upon the task of solving the problems posed at the end of the story they are not working to merely solve mathematics problems, they are working on resolving a situation within a story. Their efforts will be situated within the story context. As teachers, this gives us the power to alter, extend, and transform the dilemma to suit the needs of the class. By simply asking "what if ..." we are able to extend the mathematical context while maintaining the story context unchanged.

Again this "what if ..." is often implicit in the story itself. It lies in the script of the story and in the telling of the story as the storyteller reads both the emotional and the mathematical engagement of the audience. We have tried to make it explicit within some of the stories we have presented here. For example, in the riddle of the missing dollar we considered explicitly "what if the price of the room were different?" The presented numerical variation was the key in tackling the puzzle. In the stories of changing temperatures, of the King's diamonds, of Kathy's outfits, among others, the numerical variation is continuously present within the story.

USING EXISTING STORY BOOKS

These four elements – purpose, script, telling, and context – are an inherent and implicit part of story writing. When we engage in the writing of a story to teach mathematics we have automatic access to the affordances that they provide. When we use an existing story, however, this same access is not automatic. This is not to say that this invalidates, or makes impossible, the use of existing stories. It is only to say that if we wish to glean the same benefits from existing stories as from self-authored stories we must be aware of what is explicit and what is implicit. Attending to the aforementioned implicit elements of stories, and how we can make them explicit for our own needs will help us to utilize existing stories more effectively.

In what follows we will look at a number of existing stories, and through a consideration of purpose, script, telling, and context we will analyse the stories and show how such an analysis can help us extend their potential use in the classroom.

The Doorbell Rang by Pat Hutchins

In this classic children's book Ma has made a batch of 12 cookies for her children Victoria and Sam. Before they have a chance to share them the doorbell rings and in comes Tom and Hannah. This continues until there are 12 children in the kitchen. With each new entry there is a statement by Ma that the children "can share the cookies". This is followed by a response from Victoria and Sam as to how many cookies each child should get. Finally, when each child is getting only one cookie the doorbell rings one more time ... and in comes Grandma with a BIG batch of cookies.

It is clear that this story was written for the purpose of introducing whole number division. There are also strong indications that the story was written with some opportunity for mathematical activity in mind. Although there are no questions explicitly asked, the implication is that students have the opportunity to anticipate Victoria and Sam's answers. This is evident in the fact that the reader has to turn the page to see their answer. The context of this story is very powerful. It approaches division from a perspective of sharing and fairness that is very familiar to children. Add in the idea of cookies and friends and there is greater opportunity for heightened engagement.

So, how to use this book? At its most rudimentary level this book is a good children's story. There are powerful moral lessons regarding sharing and fairness alluded to and there is anticipation and curiosity regarding potential conflict when the doorbell rings the last time ... and there is a happy ending. From a mathematics teaching perspective there is opportunity to either introduce the notion of division through a fair share model or to reinforce and practice division by anticipating Victoria and Sam's answers. This is, of course, provided that the reader structures mathematical activity to occur as the story is being read. In the case of introducing division to young students this would require a significant break from the story at each of Ma's prompts to share the cookies to allow students to explore the scenario

CHAPTER 12

through discussion, group work, drawing, and work with manipulatives. Early in the story this may also require the reader to explicitly ask "how many cookies does each child get?" This is relatively intuitive and doesn't require deep analysis to arrive at. What is not intuitive, however, is the breadth of mathematics that this story can touch.

To begin with, this story does not necessarily have to be about whole number division. It can also be about factors. That is, what are the numbers that 12 is divisible by? If this is the mathematical content that is strived for, then the pedagogical pause needs to be inserted not when they are asked to share the cookies, but when the doorbell rings. The implicit question now becomes "how many children are at the door?" This is a subtle shift of attention that signals a significant change in student thinking. Finding factors requires much greater flexibility in thinking than doing simple division – a flexibility that can only be developed through trial and error and familiarity with division facts.

Furthermore, the context for this story is so powerful that it easily allows for extensions. By simply changing the number of cookies that Ma has baked or the number of children that come to the door we can explore the concept of division with remainder. If the numbers are carefully selected, fractions can be introduced. Consider the scenario where there are 14 cookies and 4 children. Even young children can arrive at the solution that the remaining 2 cookies can be cut in half so that each child gets 3 ½ cookies. Remainders can be further explored through the manipulation of how many cookies Grandma brings with her when she arrives. Again, twisting the standard questions can enrich these explorations – "how many children would you like to see at the door?"; "how many cookies should Ma have baked?"; "how many cookies do you hope Grandma has with her?".

Because the context of the story is so strong, and because there is such a simple rhythm to it, this story is also an excellent candidate for having children write their own version of it. They can choose their own numbers to explore or they can be asked to adhere to some set restrictions. Asking students to ensure that all factors are accounted for (by the way – in the original story, 3 is missing) or that the children in the story will always have an even number of cookies will reach further into mathematical content. Carefully selected criteria can also greatly increase the challenge of the activity. Consider the challenge of writing a story in which the doorbell rings exactly 7 times and all the factors of a number have to be accounted for. How many cookies do we need to start with?

The Doorbell Rang, as it is written, introduces a very simple mathematical concept (whole number division). *The Doorbell Rang*, as it might be read, can explore more advanced concepts (factors). *The Doorbell Rang*, as it can be altered, can examine an even more diverse set of mathematical notions (division with remainder, fractions). *The Doorbell Rang*, as it can be extended, can challenge students to engage in real mathematical thought as they work to write their own stories. Regardless of the purpose that this story was written for, the powerful context and the predictable rhythm allows us, as teachers, to easily manipulate it to meet a great many of our own purposes.

Anno's Mysterious Multiplying Jar by Masaichiro and Mitsumasa Anno

We first encountered *Anno's Mysterious Multiplying Jar* in Chapter 6 as a story that introduces a mathematical concept of factorial. In this story we are introduced to a magical jar inside of which lies a sea. And on this sea there is 1 island ... and on the island there are 2 countries ... and in each country there are 3 mountains ... and on each mountain there are 4 walled kingdoms ... and so on. As we follow the story along we encounter 5 villages (per kingdom), 6 houses (per village), 7 rooms (per house), 8 cupboards (per room), 9 boxes (per cupboard), and eventually 10 jars (per box). The *story* concludes with a question – "how many jars were in all the boxes together?". However, this is not where the *book* concludes. The authors finish by providing us the answer to their question (3,628,800 jars), as well as an explanation for how the solution is produced. They then introduce the notion of factorial and proceed to demonstrate some uses of factorial notation in combinatorics problems.

At first blush it seems as though the author's *primary* purpose in writing this book is to introduce the factorial notation. However, it is clearly not their *only* purpose. In the last sentence of the afterword they inform us that "learning about numbers and how they expand almost without limit by such simple means as are shown in this book will, we hope, give readers an idea of the remarkable order that underlies our universe, and a sense of mystery, wonder, and excitement that can be experienced through mathematics." In fact, based on the fact that there seems to be little effort to engage the reader in any mathematical activity we would argue that the authors' primary purpose is to get the reader to the mathematical explanation and elucidations about factorials, expanding numbers, and orderliness. In doing so, however, they have presented us with a wonderful context within which to play with multiplication. The idea of these nested refinements creates a meaningful space to explore what it means to have explicit and implicit quantities of things – there are 3 mountains in this country (explicit) but also in each country (implicit).

Although the authors seem driven to get to the aforementioned concepts, this book provides the skilled teacher with many opportunities to engage their students in mathematical activity. As in *The Doorbell Rang* the powerful context along with the simple rhythm of the book allows for easy exploration, alterations, and extension. Most simply, we just have to insert a question for each page – "how many mountains are there?"; "how many kingdoms are there?"; etc. As the students engage in the activities they can begin to rely on patterning to see them through. At first there may just be pattern in the process – "to figure out how many kingdoms there are we have to do the same thing as for how many mountains there are". Eventually, careful attention to the repetition within this process can allow for an emergence of the growing pattern of numbers 1, 1×2, $1\times2\times3$, $1\times2\times3\times4$, etc. Such an approach will allow even young students to answer the explicit question of how many jars there are whereas waiting to the conclusion of the story before engaging in any activity may not. At this point, an introduction to factorial notation could be made, but is not necessary.

CHAPTER 12

As mentioned, because of the rhythmical nature of the story and the now familiar context of multiplicative growth alterations to the story can be simple and rewarding. Staying with the process of solving these problems rather than the emergent number patterns we can revisit the story of the green jar (Anno's jar is blue) that was shaken a little bit. In this jar there are 3 islands, with 5 mountains on each island, and 2 kingdoms on each island, etc. Or perhaps there are 2 islands, one has 3 mountains on it and the other has 4 mountains on it, and so on. The growing complexity of such questions along with the lack of obvious number patterns necessitates additional tools to be developed. As already mentioned, careful attention to the process can be such a tool. This is important, because often in patterning type problems students lose track of the details of the task and start fixating on the number patterns that emerge. David Hewitt refers to this as 'train spotting' (Hewitt, 1992) and warns against the loss of contextual understanding that can result. Another tool that may emerge from such problems is the development of tree diagrams. Such diagrams are very useful for organizing layered information in general, and very useful when the layers are not uniform in particular.

If we want to extend the story along different curricular lines consider, for example, a different jar – a red jar. In this jar there is also a sea, but it has 2 islands. And on each island there are 2 mountains, and so on. Such a twist will allow us to introduce our students to exponential growth, exponential notation (if we wish), and special case of tree diagrams called binary trees. If we want to keep pushing we can also tell the story of the purple jar which has 5 islands and 5 mountains on each island, or of the yellow jar which has 10 islands and on each island there are 10 mountains, etc. Here we see very rapid growth and, in the case of the yellow jar, we are modelling our decimal number system. We can also ask our students to explore the relative growth rates of the four different jars (blue, red, purple, and yellow) to determine what grows faster. Here a shift to tabular and graphical representation allows for better visualization.

In the original book the authors try to link their story to combinatorics and the Fundamental Principle of Counting. They try to do this through the intermediary of factorial notation. Linking mathematical concepts only through notation is weak. In this case we can do a better job by going back to the story and rewriting it with the explicit purpose of eliciting from it the Fundamental Principle of Counting. In such a rewrite we will use the rhythm and pattern of *Anno's Mysterious Multiplying Jar* in conjunction with the Kathy's outfits problem we saw in Chapter 8. We call this story *Rina's Mysterious Multiplying Closet*.

> *This is a story about a girl and her closet.*
> *On Monday Rina went to her closet to get dressed.*
> *When she opened it the closet was empty*
> *... except for 1 dress.*
> *Oh dear, she didn't have much to wear.*

USING EXISTING STORIES

On Tuesday Rina went to her closet to get dressed.
When she opened it the closet was empty
... except for 1 dress, and 2 hats.
Oh dear, she didn't have much to wear.

On Wednesday Rina went to her closet to get dressed.
When she opened it the closet was empty
... except for 1 dress, 2 hats, and 3 belts.
Oh dear, she didn't have much to wear.

On Thursday Rina went to her closet to get dressed.
When she opened it the closet was empty
... except for 1 dress, 2 hats, 3 belts, and 4 pairs of shoes
Oh dear, she didn't have much to wear.

On Friday Rina went to her closet to get dressed.
When she opened it the closet was empty
... except for 1 dress, 2 hats, 3 belts, 4 pairs of shoes, and 5 scarves
Oh dear, she didn't have much to wear.

On Saturday Rina went to her closet to get dressed.
When she opened it the closet was empty
... except for 1 dress, 2 hats, 3 belts, 4 pairs of shoes, 5 scarves, and 6 sets of earrings
Oh dear, she didn't have much to wear.

On Sunday Rina went to her closet to get dressed.
When she opened it the closet was empty
... except for 1 dress, 2 hats, 3 belts, 4 pairs of shoes, 5 scarves, 6 sets of earrings, and 7 necklaces
Oh dear, Rina had so much to wear.

The rich contextual quality of *Anno's Mysterious Multiplying Jar* that makes this story easy to mould to our own purposes also makes this an ideal story to have students work with. As with *The Doorbell Rang* students can write their own versions of this story. This can be a freewheeling exploration and creative endeavour, or it can be a much more structured and challenging activity. Imagine the challenge of writing the story of the pink jar that has exactly 1000 pink jars inside of it. How will such a story look?

The King's Chessboard by David Birch

The storybook *The King's Chessboard* is based on an old story – the variations of which are many, and one of them is introduced in Chapter 6. The particular version that is presented in this storybook involves the King of Deccan who wishes to

CHAPTER 12

reward a wise man who has served him well. The wise man initially refuses any reward for service, but upon the King's insistence he eventually acquiesces. The reward the wise man poses is some rice to be measured out in a very specific way – "tomorrow, for the first square of your chessboard, give me one grain of rice; the next day, for the second square, two grains of rice; the next day after that, four grains of rice; then, the following day, eight grains for the next square of your chessboard. Thus for each square give me twice the number of grains of the square before it, and so on for every square of the chessboard." The story then goes on to detail the drama as the King and court laugh at the absurdity of asking only for a bit of rice, and then the drama as the daily ration of rice grows to astronomical quantities. Finally, after 32 days the King summons the wise man and concedes that he has been asked the impossible.

The story ends with the King's realization that sometimes good service is its own reward. Less forgiving versions of the story end with the wise man losing his head, thus showing that he was, perhaps, not as wise as we first thought. Many versions of the story are also more specific about the initial service that precipitated the King's desire to bestow a reward upon the wise man. Some of these versions tell of the wise man inventing the game of chess as a gift for the King, thus making the use of the chessboard in the metering out of the rice more relevant.

Clearly this story is about exponential growth. In particular, it highlights how something very small can become very big very quickly despite its initial slow growth. However, there is more to this particular version of the story. As in *Anno's Mysterious Multiplying Jar* the notion of big numbers is a central theme to the story. In fact, it is the big*ness* of the numbers that becomes the central conflict in the story. Unlike in *Anno's Mysterious Multiplying Jar*, however, this author takes a different tack in dealing with it. Rather than representing the growing amount of rice as a ridiculously long decimal place number Birch tries to relate these ever expanding quantities in contexts that are easier for students to grasp – 2048 grains becomes an ounce of rice, 16 ounces becomes a pound, pounds become a sacks, sacks become tons, and a ton becomes a wagon. In so doing the authors gives us access to another central curriculum topic – unit conversion.

In fact, this story can be read strictly from the perspective of introducing the notion of unit conversion. Although the author does not explicitly ask questions regarding unit conversions, the way in which the relationships unfold in the story gives rise to many opportunities to engage students in mathematical activity around this concept. For example, we are told that on the 12th day the Weigher concluded that 2048 grains of rice makes one ounce. We are then told that only four days later a small bag of rice was sent over "weighing 16 ounces, or one pound". A skilful story teller will leave out the detail about the 16 ounces and simply ask – "how many ounces in a pound?" Further, we then learn that only 9 days later it takes four granary workers, each carrying a large sack of rice, to deliver the days payment. Again, the unspoken question can be – "how many pounds in a sack?"

The nice feature of this story is that, in this case, we are eventually told the answer. A little more crafting and a similar question can be posed regarding the relationship between sacks and tons (it turns out to be 16 sacks to a ton). This later relationship can then be used to explore the question of how many pounds in a ton. Here some adjustment is needed as the answer comes out as 2048 pounds. In any case, the skilful use, and sometimes adjustment, in the telling of this story, along with the appropriate pauses to engage in the aforementioned mathematical activities can lead to rich learning opportunities around the topic of unit conversions.

This is not to say that we should ignore the opportunity to read the story from the perspective of exponential growth. In fact, the author's choice to invoke unit conversions make ideal the mathematical activity of actually tracking the exact quantities of rice given, each day and cumulatively, as the days go by. Such an activity will lead to the discovery that the amount that will be given on the next day is exactly one grain more than the total amount of rice given thus far. This is a property unique to the situation where the growth factor is two (i.e. it doubles every day).

Examining the amount of rice given each day can also lead to a side discussion about computer memory which is measured in bytes – *kilo*bytes, *mega*bytes, *giga*bytes, and *tera*bytes. These prefixes have very precise mathematical meanings: kilo – thousand (1000), mega – million (1,000,000), giga – billion (1,000,000,000), and tera – trillion (1,000,000,000,000). However, computer memory works on the same doubling growth model that *The King's Chessboard* presents and thus the prefixes are only approximations. One kilobyte is really 1024 bytes, one megabyte is really 1,048,576 bytes, one gigabyte is really 1,073,741,824 bytes, and one terabyte is really 1,099,511,627,776 byte – all numbers that we see if we look at how much rice is on the 11th, 21st, 31st, and 41st squares of the chessboard respectively.

Of course, looking at these numbers we can also ladder into the same activity suggested for *Anno's Mysterious Multiplying Jar* whereby the exponential growth rate is compared to the speed with which the factorial and geometric relationships grow. And of course, such an activity can serve as an introduction to the polynomial, factorial, and exponential functions.

Combining these two readings – unit conversion with cardinal quantities of rice – allows us to explore big numbers in a very effective way. Our decimal number system is so efficient in representing large quantities that it numbs us to the cardinal quantities involved. For example, 1,073,741,824 is a relatively compact number taking up no more a fraction of a line on a page of text. Stating that it represents the amount of rice that is delivered on the 31st day does not make it appear any bigger. However, when this is simultaneously represented as 16 wagons of rice a new appreciation for how big this number is begins to develop. For the most part, our students have very few opportunities to experience numbers bigger than 1000 in any meaningful way. By switching back and forth between the decimal representation and the weight/quantity representation we can begin to extend their experiences to larger numbers. Even more concretely, bringing a large bag of rice (5 or 10 kg) into class and exploring exactly how much rice is in the bag will add even more meaning to such a reading of the story.

CHAPTER 12

Sir Cumference and the Dragon of Pi by Cindy Neuschwander

This is the story of *Sir Cumference*, a knight who is magically turned into a fire breathing dragon, and his son Radius who must somehow turn him back into a man before he is slain by the other knights. On his quest, Radius unlocks the secret relationship between the circumference and the diameter of a circle – which turns out to be the *exact* quantity of magic potion he must administer to his dragon father. Of course, this secret relationship is $\pi = 3.14159...$ or approximately 22/7.

This is a clever story that, although it has no explicit questions, presents a context that is so inviting that it is a simple matter to turn it into some mathematical activities. There is a particularly clever treatment of this issue on page 17 of the story in which Radius explores how many diameters fit around the circumference of the circle. Radius also finds other ways to explore the relationship – each of which can be extended to a classroom activity.

There is something in this story that we haven't seen in any of the other stories we have looked at – something that can be used as an introduction to an activity of a different sort. This story is written using a tongue-in-cheek humour regarding the names of many of the characters, as well as some of the circumstances Radius finds himself in. From the two brothers Geo and Sym of Metry to the fact that Radius finds himself doing explorations with pies, the author has riddled the story with clever little relationships between mathematical words, values, and definitions. As mentioned in the chapter on humour, such use of language requires deep understanding of mathematical concepts. Thus, we see this story as a good model for having students write their own tongue-in-cheek stories in which they too can play with mathematical terminology.

Jayden's Rescue by Vladimir Tumanov

Jayden's Rescue is story that involves the adventures of Alex and his friends as they work to free Jayden who is held captive in a castle made up of 400 rooms, each guarded by a monster, each of whom poses the young adventurers a new mathematics problem. The plot of the story is ingenious, beginning with Alex's discovery of a magic pencil and a book that is more than just a book. As Alex reads he begins to realize that the main character, Jayden, is more than a just a character in a story and her plight is more than just fiction. The reader is drawn into Alex's adventure in the same way Alex is drawn into Jayden's troubles.

Although the plot mentions 400 rooms the reader is not charged with the task of navigating all 400. However, the story does take us through many rooms and introduces us to many monster guards and many mathematics problems each one unique and distinct from those already encountered. Each problem would be well suited for a middle school classroom with some requiring knowledge of fractions and others requiring a bit of algebra. All of the problems touch curriculum content in one way or another and each can be used as the impetus to classroom activity. Even the requirement that the answers to each problem be written down and handed to the monster feeds right into suitable classroom activity.

This story is a classic case of a story that introduces a problem, albeit an extended one, in that the story context itself has little to do with the problems posed. Thus, the problems could be swapped out for any problem a teacher may wish their students to engage in. However, the author has gone to great length to present the problems in interesting fashions (rhyme, riddles, etc.) that would be difficult to replicate should the problems be changed.

Again, this story sets a good template for students perhaps writing their own versions. A very reasonable assignment would be to have students write about some of the rooms the story does not take us into. This would give them a chance to be creative about the type of monsters that may roam there as well as the type of grisly consequence a wrong answer may garnish, all the while giving students the opportunity to showcase the mathematics that they may find interesting.

The Number Devil by Hans Magnus Enzensberger

The Number Devil is similar to *Jayden's Rescue* in that it is an extended story used to introduce mathematics that has nothing to do with the plot. Unlike *Jayden's Rescue*, however, the mathematics is far too interwoven into the story to simply extract it and replace it with mathematics of a different sort.

In this story, Robert, a boy who hates mathematics encounters a dream character who introduces him to the wonderful world of numbers. Through 12 dreams Robert meets triangular numbers, square numbers, Fibonacci numbers, the Pascal triangle, and so on. Unlike Jayden's Rescue, the plot is very much secondary to the mathematics here – and the mathematics goes far beyond posing of problems to explaining solutions and properties. Although there are many problems and activities implicit in the telling of the story there are also very explicitly stated problems and activities at the end of each chapter/dream. Again, the context is all laid out for thoughtful engagement of the students, and again skilful telling is required to extract the full potential of this book.

The Math Curse by Jon Scieszka and Lane Smith

The Math Curse is a simple story of how one little girl can't avoid seeing mathematics everywhere she looks. The book is full of explicitly posed questions that can be turned into student activity. Although the questions start out simple enough the difficulty quickly escalates as the reader/listener is taken through an expansive number of mathematical topics from measurement to binary notation to logic. Along the way we also meet a number of nonsensical questions such as "why doesn't February have a w?", as well as problems that require a large amount of very sensible estimation to solve such as "estimate how many M&M's it would take to measure the Mississippi River". On a grander scale, this story also effectively demonstrates that mathematics is all around us if we only open our eyes to it.

Aside from using the book as a nice introduction to some very clever problems, and hence some very good mathematical activity, the book also provides an excellent template for students to create their own math curse adventures. Our experiences with such an activity have been very rewarding. It not only signals to students that they themselves can detect mathematics in the world around them, it also gives students the freedom to showcase the mathematics that they see as interesting in very creative ways. Even the illustration style of the book is something that students can easily copy as they work to write their own *Math Curse*.

RESOURCES

We have looked at seven stories here, some in more details than other. But these are only seven out of many, many, many stories. There are thousands of potential stories that a classroom teacher could choose from to teach mathematics. There are also annotated collections, some with explicit relationship to curriculum topics (e.g. Burns, 1995; Griffiths & Clyne, 1991; Schiro, 2004; Thiessen, 2004; Thiessen & Matthias, 1992; Ward, 2009).

The message we have tried to communicate here is that it takes more than just locating such stories to have successful mathematical encounters. The teacher needs to be aware of the author's purpose in writing the story, and then make full use of script, context, and telling in order to shape the story to fit his or her own particular need.

Aside from the existence of these many stories there also many resources that may help teachers to select and use stories for the teaching of mathematics. Some of the resources exist in webpages, others in books. Some resources are merely lists of stories, others are lists categorized by mathematics topic. Other resources focus more on aiding teachers to integrate mathematics with other content areas through the use of stories.

Due to the changing nature of webpages and ever increasing amount of print resources, we resist the temptation to provide the reader with the list. However, we believe that every storyteller has such a list, if not on paper, then in his/her heart. We hope that this book gets included on at least some of these lists.

REFERENCES

Anno, M., & Anno, M. (1983). *Anno's mysterious multiplying jar*. New York, NY: Philomel Books.
Baker, A., & Greene, E. (1987). *Storytelling: Art and technique*. New York, NY: R.R. Bowker Company.
Ball, D. (1990). Prospective elementary and secondary teacher's understanding of division. *Journal for Research in Mathematics Education, 21*, 132-144.
Balakrishnan, C. (2008). *Teaching secondary school mathematics through storytelling*. Unpublished MSc thesis. Simon Fraser University.
Bauer, C. F. (1993). *New handbook for storytellers*. Chicago, IL: American Library Association.
Bettelheim, B. (1976). *The uses of enchantment: Meaning and importance of fairy tales*. New York, NY: Knopf.
Birch, D. (1993). *The king's chessboard*. New York, NY: Puffin Books.
Brown, D. (2006). *Angels and demons*. New York, NY: Washington Square Press.
Burns, M. (1995). *Writing in math class*. Sausalito, CA: Math Solutions Publications.
Burrell, A. (1926/1971). *A guide to story telling*. Ann Arbor, MI: Grypton Books.
Cohen, T. (1999). *Jokes: Philosophical thoughts on joking matters*. Chicago, IL: University of Chicago Press.
Demi (1997). *One grain of rice*. New York, NY: Scholastic Press.
Dewey, J. (1913) *Interest and Effort in Education*. Cambridge, Mass: Riverside Press.
Egan, K. (1986). *Teaching as story telling: An alternative approach to teaching and curriculum in the elementary school*. Chicago, IL: University of Chicago Press.
Egan, K. (1997). *The educated mind: How cognitive tools shape our understanding*. Chicago, IL: University of Chicago Press.
Egan, K. (2004). The cognitive tools of children's imagination. *Early Childhood Education, 36*(1), 4-10.
Egan, K. (2008). *Cognitive tools and imagination*. Available: http://www.educ.sfu.ca/kegan/Cognitive_tools_and_imagin.html
Enzensberger, H. M. (1997). *The number devil*. New York, NY: Owl Books.
Green, M. C. (2004). Storytelling in teaching. *Observer, 17*(4). Available: http://www.psychologicalscience.org/observer/getArticle.cfm?id=1562
Griffiths, R., & Clyne, M. (1991). *Books you can count on: Linking mathematics and literature*. Portsmouth, NH: Heinemann.
Haven, K. (2000). *Super simple storytelling: A can-do guide for every classroom, every day*. Englewood, CO: Teacher Ideas Press.
Hewitt, D. (1992). Train spotters' paradise. *Mathematics Teaching, 140*, 6–8.
Hofstadter, D. (1980). *Gödel, Escher, Bach: An eternal golden braid*. New York, NY: Basic Books.
Hutchins, P. (1986). *The doorbell rang*. New York, NY: Mulberry Books.
Johnson, B., (2000). *A story is a promise: Good things to know before you write that screenplay, novel, or play*. Portland, OR: Blue Haven Publishing.
Mason, J. (1996). Expressing generality and roots of algebra. In N. Bednarz, C. Kieran, & L. Lee (Eds.), *Approaches to algebra: Perspectives for research and teaching* (pp. 65-86). Dordrecht, Netherlands: Kluwer.
Mason, J. (2001). Tunja Sequences as example of employing students; power to generalize. *Mathematics Teacher, 94*(3), 164-169.
Mason, J. (2007). *Structured variation grids*. Available: http://msc.open.ac.uk/jhm3/

REFERENCES

Mason, J. & Pimm, D. (1984). Generic examples: Seeing the general in the particular. *Educational Studies in Mathematics, 15,* 277-289.

National Council of Teachers of Mathematics (NCTM). (1989) *Historical topics for the mathematics classroom.* Reston, VA: NCTM.

National Council of Teachers of Mathematics (NCTM). (2000). *Principles and standards for school mathematics.* Reston, VA: NCTM.

Neuschwander, C. (1999). *Sir Cumference and the Dragon of Pi.* Watertown, MA: Charlesbridge Publishing, Inc.

Pappas, T. (1991). *More joy of mathematics.* San Carlos: Wide World Publishing/Tetra.

Paulos, J. A. (1982). *Mathematics and humor: A study of the logic of humor.* Chicago, IL: University of Chicago Press.

Pellowsky, A. (1977). *The world of storytelling.* New York, NY: R.R. Bowker Company.

Polya, G. (1945/1988). *How to solve it.* Princeton, NJ: Princeton University Press.

Rucker, R. (1999). A new golden age. In W. Frucht (Ed.). *Imaginary numbers: an anthology of marvellous mathematical stories, diversions, poems and musings* (pp.11-19). New York, NY: John Wiley & Sons.

Scieszka, J., & Smith, L. (1995). *Math curse.* New York, NY: Penguin Books.

Shedlock, M. (1924). *The art of the story-teller.* New York, NY: D. Appleton and Company.

Schiro, M. S. (2004). *Oral storytelling & teaching mathematics.* Thousand Oaks, CA: Sage Publications.

Stavy, R., & Tirosh, D. (2000). *How students (mis-)understand science and mathematics: Intuitive rules.* New York: Teachers College Press.

Tahan, M. (1972). *The man who counted.* New York, NY: W.W. Norton & Company.

Thiessen, D. (Ed.) (2004). *Exploring mathematics through literature: Articles and lessons from prekindergarten through Grade 8.* Reston, VA: NCTM.

Thiessen, D., & Matthias, M. (Eds.) (1992). *The wonderful world of mathematics: A critically annotated list of children's books in mathematics.* Reston, VA: NCTM.

Tompert, A., & Parker, R. A. (1997). *Grandfather's Tang's story.* Albuquerque, New Mexico: Dragonfly Books.

Tumanov, V. (2002). *Jayden's rescue.* Markham, Ontario: Scholastic Canada.

Ward, R. A. (2009). *Literature-based activities for integrating mathematics with other content areas.* New York, NY: Pearson.